The Old College Try
Balancing Academics and Athletics in Higher Education

by John R. Thelin and Lawrence L. Wiseman

ASHE-ERIC Higher Education Report 4, 1989

D0140254

Prepared by

Clearinghouse on Higher Education
The George Washington University

In cooperation with

ASHE

Association for the Study
of Higher Education

Published by

School of Education and Human Development
The George Washington University

Jonathan D. Fife, Series Editor

Cite as

Thelin, John R. and Lawrence L. Wiseman. *The Old College Try: Balancing Athletics and Academics in Higher Education.* Report No. 4. Washington, D.C.: School of Education and Human Development, The George Washington University, 1989.

Library of Congress Catalog Card Number 89-63440
ISSN 0884-0040
ISBN 0-9623882-3-8

Managing Editor: Christopher Rigaux
Manuscript Editor: Barbara Fishel/Editech
Cover design by Michael David Brown, Rockville, Maryland

The ERIC Clearinghouse on Higher Education invites individuals to submit proposals for writing monographs for the *ASHE-ERIC Higher Education Report* series. Proposals must include:
1. A detailed manuscript proposal of not more than five pages.
2. A chapter-by-chapter outline.
3. A 75-word summary to be used by several review committees for the initial screening and rating of each proposal.
4. A vita and a writing sample.

ERIC **Clearinghouse on Higher Education**
School of Education and Human Development
The George Washington University
One Dupont Circle, Suite 630
Washington, DC 20036-1183

This publication was prepared partially with funding from the Office of Educational Research and Improvement, U.S. Department of Education, under contract no. ED RI-88-062014. The opinions expressed in this report do not necessarily reflect the positions or policies of OERI or the Department.

EXECUTIVE SUMMARY

A decade of highly publicized sports scandals at several major universities has made intercollegiate athletics a serious matter that academic leaders can no longer afford to ignore. Beyond the publicity of violated rules is a less obvious, fundamental problem affecting the health of American colleges and universities: Standard procedures and policies of intercollegiate athletics often conflict with sound institutional planning. The most dangerous game today in college sports is the financial strategy that leaves even big-time athletics programs overextended and fragile. And along with lack of financial control, many intercollegiate athletics programs are only marginally connected to academic accountability.

The Old College Try brings intercollegiate sports to the center of research and discussion about higher education. Its premise is that policy regarding athletics should be understood as integral to educational mission, philosophy, and structure. College sports are a matter of public policy, academic governance, institutional finance, and economics.

What Are the Business and Politics of College Sports?

An analysis of the relationship between sound business practices and the finances of big-time intercollegiate athletics indicates that most budgets for athletics programs show signs of precarious fiscal fitness. Over the past decade, an alarming syndrome has evolved: a rich-get-richer pattern, with an increasing number of major programs showing deficits. Despite large crowds and widespread publicity, few athletics programs are self-supporting because rising expenses continually jump ahead of revenues. And, athletics directors and coaches have tended to vote against reforms that would contain costs. Television revenues assist only a small number of institutions— with little prospect for increased net revenues. Varsity sports programs that show deficits look to private donations and mandatory student fees as strategies for balancing budgets, usually through the mechanism of specially incorporated athletic foundations, entities that tend to drift away from academic accountability.

Such practices move analysis from institutional finance to public policy. The key finding of the research is that some standard procedures of big-time sports programs jeopardize many privileges and exemptions colleges traditionally have enjoyed as nonprofit educational organizations. Sports programs managed as admittedly commercial enterprises tend to have government agencies looking at athletic foundations more as entertainment than as education. Thus, athletic foundations may have to forfeit exemptions from local property tax. Second, the IRS will increasingly scrutinize athletic foundations' activities and expenses to determine whether they should be exempt from federal income taxes. Donors will be less likely to claim tax deductions for donations to athletics programs that have little demonstrable connection with an institution's educational mission.

Why Do College Sports Programs Resist Reform?

Given these economic and policy problems, why do intercollegiate athletics programs resist academic reform? Observers agree that the key figure in such reform is the college or university president. Yet making decisive changes in athletics policy is not easy for a president who must contend with external pressures, problems of a single campus working in isolation, and the visibility of college sports. Presidents who take a stand as national leaders and spokesmen on containing the costs and abuses of college sports show a high burnout rate. Above all, a president must work within the boundaries of an institution's sports heritage. Justification for big-time sports programs includes the claim that college sports bring prestige, publicity, and donations that benefit the entire institution—leading to spirited debates among social and political scientists who have attempted to systematically test such claims.

Changing policy is complicated because many important actions and attempts at reform take place beyond the campus. The really exciting contests in varsity sports are taking place not on the playing fields but in the courts, in college board rooms, at NCAA conventions, in presidents' offices, and at television network headquarters. Significant reform most likely will not come about until standards for intercollegiate athletics programs are recognized as central to an institution's mission—and hence subject to prominent scrutiny in regional accreditation.

What Reform Measures Can Help Achieve a Proper Balance between Academics and Athletics?

To balance academics and athletics, reforms in the following areas are recommended:

- *Institutional mission statement:* If intercollegiate sports are de facto central—not peripheral—to a university's purpose, it should be so stated forthrightly as a de jure dimension. It is no idle exercise if the mission statement is used in substantive institutional evaluation, for example, in regional accreditation.
- *Regional accreditation standards:* Standards could be revised so as to make intercollegiate athletics a distinct category of total institutional self-study rather than obscured as an adjunct to, say, "student affairs." Thus, a university that failed to comply with its self-determined standard for intercollegiate athletics would jeopardize its accredited status for the *entire* institution.
- *Collective solutions and self-regulation:* The best strategies for a sound policy regarding athletics involve cooperation among colleges and their presidents. Advocates of a recurrent proposal to deregulate the "business" of college sports invoke the principle of institutional self-determination, suggesting that effective centralized and uniform regulation by a national body is unlikely. But economic deregulation probably would lead to the financial collapse of most varsity sports programs, even those in the NCAA's Division I. A better solution than deregulation would be *self-*regulation. Although the diversity of American higher education renders *national* policies unwieldy, the *conference* has great potential for peer institutions to cooperate voluntarily and with mutual respect. Foremost items for collective consideration should be the reduction of expenses by such measures as reducing the number of permissible athletic grants-in-aid and by making all grants-in-aid based on financial need.
- *Internal taxation:* Institutions with major revenue-producing athletics programs should consider charging overhead expenses on each dollar of revenue or philanthropy generated by intercollegiate athletics programs. Doing so would formally ensure, as claimed by varsity sports advocates, that athletic fund raising is for the benefit of the entire institution.
- *Governance:* While emphasizing the real and symbolic role of the campus president in intercollegiate athletics, leadership can best be demonstrated by *selective* and *discriminating* presidential involvement. Emphasis should

be on policy matters involving the presidents of other colleges and universities. Institutions are therefore urged to make good use of campus administrative expertise beyond the president: for example, depending on whether a college chooses to emphasize the educational or the business dimension of varsity sports, one might opt to have the athletics director report to the academic vice president in the former case or to the vice president for business affairs in the latter.

- *Public policy for nonprofit organizations:* Intercollegiate athletics programs that define themselves as a business and are incorporated as a foundation distinct from the university should be prepared to have local governments and the IRS treat them as commercial enterprises rather than as nonprofit educational activities.

- *Structure:* Semiautonomous athletic foundations should be disbanded and replaced with a departmental structure within institutional administrative and financial control. Otherwise, athletics directors report to both an institutional office and to a foundation board, thus diluting presidential and academic oversight.

ADVISORY BOARD

Roger G. Baldwin
Assistant Professor of Education
College of William and Mary

Carol M. Boyer
Consultant and Senior Academic Planner
Massachusetts Board of Regents of Higher Education

Ellen Earle Chaffee
Associate Commissioner of Academic Affairs
North Dakota State Board of Higher Education

Martin Finkelstein
Associate Professor of Higher Education Administration
Seton Hall University

Carol Everly Floyd
Associate Vice Chancellor for Academic Affairs
Board of Regents of the Regency Universities System
State of Illinois

George D. Kuh
Professor of Higher Education
Indiana University

Yvonna S. Lincoln
Associate Professor of Higher Education
University of Kansas

Michael A. Olivas
Professor of Law
University of Houston

Richard F. Wilson
Associate Chancellor
University of Illinios

Ami Zusman
Principal Analyst, Academic Affairs
University of California

CONSULTING EDITORS

Robert Berdahl
Professor of Higher Education
University of Maryland

L. Leon Campbell
Provost and Vice President for Academic Affairs
University of Delaware

Darrell Clowes
Associate Professor of Education
Viginia Tech

Susan Cohen
Associate, Project for Collaborative Learning
Lesley College

John W. Creswell
Professor and Lilly Project Director
University of Nebraska

Andre Deruyttere
Vice President
Catholic University at Leuven, Belgium

Mary E. Dilworh
Director, Research and Information Services
ERIC Clearinghouse on Teacher Education

Lawrence Erickson
Professor and Coordinator of Reading and Language Studies
Southern Illinois University

Irwin Feller
Director, Institute for Policy Research and Evaluation
Pennsylvania State University

J. Wade Gilley
Senior Vice President
George Mason University

Kenneth C. Green
Associate Director
Higher Education Research Institute
University of California at Los Angeles

Milton Greenberg
Provost
American University

Judith Dozier Hackman
Associate Dean
Yale University

Brian L. Hawkins
Vice President for Computing and Information Sciences
Brown University

Lynn G. Johnson
Executive Director
Hudson-Mohawk Association of Colleges and Universities

Carl J. Lange
Professor Emeritus
The George Washington University

Oscar T. Lenning
Vice President for Academic Affairs
Robert Wesleyan College

Judith B. McLaughlin
Research Associate on Education and Sociology
Harvard University

Andrew T. Masland
Judicial/Public Safety Market Manager
Digital Equipment Corporation

James R. Mingle
Executive Director
State Higher Education Executive Officers

Christopher B. Morris
Director of Athletics
Davidson College

Elizabeth M. Nuss
Executive Director
National Association of Student Personnel Administrators

Jeffrey H. Orleans
Executive Director
Council of Ivy Group Presidents

Wayne Otto
Professor of Curriculum and Instruction
University of Wisconsin

Anne M. Pratt
Director for Foundation Relations
College of William and Mary

John E. Roueche
Professor and Director
Community College Leadership Program
Sid W. Richardson Regents Chair
University of Texas

Mary Ellen Sheridan
Director of Sponsored Programs Administration
Ohio State University

William F. Stier, Jr.
Professor and Director of Intercollegiate Athletics
State University of New York at Brockport

Betty Taylor
Coordinator, Office of Educational Policy
New Jersey Department of Higher Education

J. Fredericks Volkwein
Director of Institutional Research
State University of New York at Albany

Reginald Wilson
Senior Scholar
American Council on Education

CONTENTS

FOREWORD

Everyone feels good when you have a winning team. But as the old adage goes, we win, they lose. No one wants to be associated with the corruption and scandal that all too frequently has been connected with college athletics. However, the controversy surrounding collegiate athletics is more than just a concern over public relations. The issue is not whether there is good news or bad news, but whether there can be a successful co-existence between the differing beliefs and values that exist between athletics and an institution's educational mission.

It is too simplistic to take the position that if an activity does not contribute to the intellectual growth of a student than it doesn't belong as part of the institution. Obviously, there are many activites that contribute to the total college experience, which on their own may not appear to be essential to the institution.

What makes athletics so controversial? It is not the activity itself, but its potential to affect so much the rest of the institution. Among the issues are:

- *Finances:* In periods of restricted funding, non-academic expenses are seen as inappropriately diverting funds away from the institution's educational activities.
- *Academic favoritism:* When student-athletes appear to have a more important non-academic role, there is always a suspicion that academic standards will be corrupted in order to insure that the non-academic role is undisturbed.
- *Power:* When non-academic activities appear to be more popular and therefore more influential, there is always a fear that the educational mission will take a secondary position.

It is a concern with the sum total of these issues that has led John Thelin and Lawrence Wiseman, both of the College of William and Mary, to pen this timely and forthright monograph. The authors note the variety of methods available to curb abuses in athletics departments, with supporting roles available for faculty and administrators alike.

Two facts seem to have received universal agreement: First, that athletics has, does, and probably will play a major positive role and second, that the higher education administrators need to have greater awareness and control over the role that athletics take at their institution. This report will provide assistance to those concerned individuals that want to play a positive role in the relationship between education and sports.

Jonathan D. Fife
Professor and Director
ERIC Clearinghouse on Higher Education
School of Education and Human Development
The George Washington University

ACKNOWLEDGEMENTS

Intercollegiate athletics has proven to be a popular topic within the higher education community. We are pleasantly surprised at the number of higher education leaders who have responded enthusiastically to our inquiries to give insights and recommendations for extending our network of correspondents and discussants. Our research has gained immensely from the information and interpretations of colleagues and correspondents at colleges, universities, and associations throughout the nation. A generous grant from the Spencer Foundation provided time for research on the historical context of intercollegiate athletics and for our final editing of the manuscript during summer 1989.

If intercollegiate athletics is a popular topic, it is also volatile. Our inquiries and discussions often have included strong opinions and even stronger differences of opinion. Those who cooperated with our interviews do not necessarily endorse our policy recommendations. We acknowledge our scholarly debt to others and at the same time take responsibility for the limits of our presentation. The interpretations we present in *The Old College Try* are our own. If they elicit disagreement and controversy, we hope it will be in the spirit of healthy debate. Jonathan Fife, series editor, and Christopher Rigaux, managing editor, of the Higher Education Report series provided timely suggestions that have strengthened our analysis, and Barbara Fishel, working with the editorial staff, skillfully copy edited the manuscript. Thoughtful, detailed commentary by four outside reviewers enhanced our thinking about college sports.

We owe special thanks to George Hanford, president emeritus of the College Entrance Examination Board, whose research in the 1970s has been instrumental in bringing college sports to the national higher education agenda. Robert Atwell, president of the American Council on Education, has been interested and supportive. Sheldon Steinbach, legal counsel for the American Council on Education, alerted us to the superb scholarly work on the topic by Arthur Padilla of the University of North Carolina, whose patient elaborations on his economic research helped make our literature review timely. Chancellor Ira Michael Heyman of the University of California–Berkeley found time in a characteristically busy schedule to talk at length about the problems and prospects of nationwide athletics reform.

President John T. Casteen of the University of Connecticut

pointed us to key people and sources, while also providing glimpses of the complexities a university president faces in dealing with intercollegiate athletics as an integral matter of institutional life. Robert M. Rosenzweig, president of the Association of American Universities, has been a long-time correspondent and commentator on sports, college and professional. Professor Jack Schuster of Claremont Graduate School likewise personifies the prominent place that college sports can have in the work and play of serious scholars. It is no accident that one of our most fruitful conversations about athletics policy took place at a historic football game between William and Mary and Princeton. The complicated external "third factors" that impinge on budgetary analysis were most evident as we talked while watching the Princeton band leave the stadium playing "Back to Old Nassau."

Much of the information in our case studies draws from public policy and institutional examples from Virginia, certainly reflecting our own geographical location. But at the same time, by coincidence, Virginia has turned out to be a significant place for events of national importance. We owe special thanks to Dr. Andrew Fogarty, secretary of administration, for his concise, candid, and perceptive insights on state government and intercollegiate athletics; he kindly provided us information on Governor Gerald Baliles's landmark commencement address in 1987 at Virginia Tech. Gordon K. Davies, director of the State Council of Higher Education for Virginia, has been a leading spokesperson on the issue of student fees and intercollegiate athletics policy. He aided our research with generous conversations and access to nationwide data from the SHEEO network.

Our own roles at The College of William and Mary as, respectively, chair and member of the Athletic Policy Advisory Committee, have provided us good opportunity to listen to and learn from some astute participant-observers in the games that colleges play. We are especially grateful to President Paul Verkuil; former President Thomas A. Graves, Jr., now director of Winterthur Museum; Athletic Director John Randolph; Associate Athletic Director Milly West; and Assistant Athletic Director George Storck. Stephen D. Harris of Williamsburg has been a knowledgeable commentator from the multiple perspectives of student-athlete, alumnus, and attorney. James Copeland, formerly athletics director at William and Mary and now athletics director at the University of Virginia, generously assisted us with information about those institutions and examples drawn from his experience at the University of Missouri and the University of Utah.

Coauthor Wiseman spent the 1987–88 academic year as an American Council on Education fellow, with assignment as special assistant to Dr. E. Gordon Gee, president of the University of Colorado. As part of that assignment, President Gee and then Assistant Vice President for Budget and Finance Joseph J. Geiger took time to talk about the study. Other members of the faculty and staff at the University of Colorado who were especially helpful include Athletic Director Bill Marolt, Associate Athletic Director Jon F. Burianek, Special Assistant to the President Adam Goodman, and Professor William H. Baughn, NCAA faculty representative.

Our close colleague, Professor Roger Baldwin of William and Mary, read drafts of the manuscript and thoughtfully steered us to key works that strengthened our discussion of presidents, faculty, and governance in higher education. We owe special thanks to our families for their encouragement and support on this project. A. Sharon Thelin generously assisted in editing the manuscript and suggesting entries for the bibliography. Leo Murphy, combining the roles of coauthor Wiseman's father-in-law and trainer for the Cleveland Browns, enriched the research with almost 40 years of experience to shape his observations about the world of professional sports.

One residual message is that intercollegiate athletics does have many friends who hold positions of academic and educational leadership. We think it is fair to say that most of our colleagues have some variation of dissenting loyalty about the condition of college sports. Our common concern is less with dismantling than with saving intercollegiate athletics. The task is important and deserves no less than the old college try.

To Eugene Leach, coach and teacher
And
To Nancy, for her support and understanding

ACADEMICS AND ATHLETICS: Probing a Precarious Balance

Intercollegiate Athletics:
The Perils of Publicity

A truism for colleges and universities is that national publicity is the lifeblood of institutional prestige (Flexner 1930; Slosson 1910; Veysey 1964). Nowhere is this article of faith more evident than in the resources American campuses dedicate to visible, successful varsity teams (Nelson 1982, p. 53). Zealous supporters of college sports, however, often overlook the pitfalls of publicity. Colleges that seek prestige through major athletics programs are especially susceptible to the curse, "May all your dreams come true at an early age." College sports have been incredibly successful in attracting publicity— but often this celebration turns sour, becoming justifiably unfavorable visibility (Frey 1982, p. 7).

Big-time college athletics had moved from the sports page to the front page— and the news was not good.

A case study illustrates the fickle life cycle of publicity about college sports. On January 4, 1985, a feature story in *The Washington Post* hailed intercollegiate athletics at Virginia Polytechnic Institute and State University for having achieved national success in both football and basketball and cited the athletics program, ascending "within shouting range of the best," for its distinctive financial and administrative arrangement (Hardie 1985). Praise was perhaps premature, for over the next three years the intercollegiate athletics department at the school was the source of controversy that brought *unfavorable* news coverage and internal strain to the entire institution. Big-time college athletics had moved from the sports page to the front page—and the news was not good. A chronology of events over two years shows that:

- The athletics director/football coach resigned when his contract as athletics director was not renewed.
- The National Collegiate Athletic Association (NCAA) cited the football and basketball teams for serious violations of recruiting practices and eligibility. An audit showed that during a three-year period Virginia Tech had exceeded its allowable number of athletics grants-in-aid by 37.
- Virginia Tech administrators were reported to have received free trips and special car deals through the university athletics association.
- The basketball coach resigned in the wake of controversy over recruiting violations.
- The governor of Virginia focused on criticism of over-

emphasis on varsity sports at his commencement speech at Virginia Tech in June 1987.

- Admissions records showed that Virginia Tech athletes' average SAT scores were more than 400 points below the institution's norm of 1080.
- In July 1987, the athletics program was $4 million in debt.
- The university's athletics fund-raising corporation was dissolved, and oversight and control of intercollegiate athletics were placed within the university's formal administrative structure.

Problems in the athletics program coincided with the university president's resignation. The irony of this saga about publicity is that in November 1987 a small news article buried in the back announced that the interim president sought a "new image for Virginia Tech" as he traveled the state "in an effort to repair the university's tarnished image" (Associated Press 1987c). The manifesto did not emphasize big-time varsity sports, illustrating Goethe's admonition, "Hell is truth discovered too late."

If the sports events at Virginia Tech were unusual, they were hardly unique (Hardy and Berryman 1982, p. 15). During the past five years, a number of prominent American universities, including Southern Methodist University, Tulane, the University of Southern California, the University of San Francisco, Clemson, the University of Maryland, the University of Kentucky, the University of Minnesota, the University of Illinois, the University of Oklahoma, and Oklahoma State University, had their own exposes in which abuses associated with intercollegiate athletics brought unfavorable national publicity. A check of feature articles or cover stories in national publications like *The Wall Street Journal, U.S. News and World Report,* and *Sports Illustrated* indicates that "scandal" has been the dominant image for college sports (Frey 1982; Merritt 1985; Thelin 1981).

The tendency is to dismiss or isolate intercollegiate athletics as a peripheral activity, not especially germane to the primary purposes of higher education (Nelson 1982, pp. 52–54). But it is an unsatisfactory excuse. First, intercollegiate athletics has become both conspicuous and substantial, resulting in a presence that cannot be overlooked (Hanford 1976; Savage et al. 1929). Second, the national publicity associated with scandals at a handful of universities with big-time varsity sports programs has a disproportionate influence on public images and opinions of *all* colleges and universities. The media attention afforded big games and big scandals dominates and distorts the popular image of what American higher education is all about. The most serious concern is that flagrant, sustained abuses in college sports programs lead to the erosion of public faith in institutions of higher education. No college or university president is exempt from the harmful effects of such eroding confidence. But above all, the disproportionate coverage given to varsity sports even *without* scandal is imbalanced (Michener 1976, pp. 219–80).

These institutional examples suggest that leaders in higher education no longer have adequate grounds to ignore intercollegiate athletics in our conception of the place of higher education in American society. The best evidence is that presidents do indeed get fired over disputes about varsity sports. Policy about athletics is closely connected to an institution's educational philosophy, mission, and structure (Hanford 1976), and as such, it deserves serious attention.

Varsity sports in American higher education is a paradox (Scott 1956, pp. 29–30). On the one hand, the topic receives relatively little attention in the formal, scholarly studies of higher education administration and governance. For example, it receives no topical inclusion in the annual *Higher Education Bibliography Yearbook* (Halstead 1987). Papers presented at the annual conferences of the Association for the Study of Higher Education over the past decade show virtually no concern with intercollegiate athletics as a policy issue. A widely used reference work, *The Assessment of College Performance* (Miller 1979), presents thoughtful chapters on systematic monitoring of numerous campus offices and functions ranging from admissions to development but no mention of intercollegiate athletics as a discrete area of institutional assessment. The scholarly literature on governance and presidencies deals with problems of decision making in a generic manner. An important exception is *The Governance of Intercollegiate Athletics* (Frey 1982), but apart from this volume, only scant and scattered mention has focused on college sports as a distinctive, significant topic. In contrast, intercollegiate sports stands prominently as the dimension of college and university activity receiving the most coverage in the national, regional, and local media. The intent of this study is to redress this imbalance—to review and analyze scholarly literature so as to foster serious interest in intercollegiate athletics as a central part of the character and operation of American colleges and universities.

Trends in Research and Scholarship

If serious analysis of college sports policy has suffered benign neglect, it is still important to note that the higher education community is indebted to some thoughtful writers and researchers for having analyzed issues involving college sports. Fifteen years ago, George Hanford (1974a, 1974b) undertook a comprehensive study that is invaluable for both reference and inspired inquiry. In 1976, James Michener's *Sports in America* picked up on Hanford's work for Michener's own thoughtful exploration of key episodes dealing with problems in varsity sports at institutions both large and small. Robert Atwell (1979, 1985, 1988) at the American Council on Education raised interest in the topic in his dual roles as an economist and as president of ACE. Several journals have devoted special issues to the topic—the *Journal of College and University Law* (1983–84), *Educational Record* (1979), *The College Board Review* (1978), *Academe* (1987)—and since 1985 *The Chronicle of Higher Education* has featured a major section in each issue on intercollegiate athletics. Most recently, L. Jay Oliva (1989) of New York University wrote a special report for the Association of Governing Boards of Universities and Colleges, *What Trustees Should Know about Intercollegiate Athletics.* Perhaps now is the time these sparks will catch. This review and synthesis of the literature, as well as fresh data and insights, are intended to continue this persistent effort.

The list of references is sprinkled with enduring scholarly works. A heartening sign in the past few years is that the topic of intercollegiate athletics has attracted good, interesting studies from the perspectives of economics, political science, geography, sociology, and law. Worth special note are "On the Economics of Intercollegiate Athletic Programs" (Padilla and Boucher 1987–88), *The Money Game: Financing Collegiate Athletics* (Atwell, Grimes, and Lopiano 1980), and *The Political Economy of College Sports* (Hart-Nibbrig and Cottingham 1986). For a provocative analysis based on "cartel theory," timely studies include "The Intercollegiate Sport Cartel and Its Consequences for Athletes" (Sage 1982) and *Unsportsmanlike Conduct: The National Collegiate Athletic*

Association and the Business of College Football (Lawrence 1987b). *The Recruiting Game* (Rooney 1987) contains thorough and imaginative studies of regional and institutional trends in the import-export commerce of collegiate athletic talent and stands as a model of exciting scholarship whose recommendations for reform would drastically alter the structure and finances of college sports. *Sport and Higher Education* (Chu, Segrave, and Becker 1985) is a useful anthology of sociological research monographs, and "Legal Accountability and the NCAA" (Weistart 1983–84), "College Sports Reform" (Weistart 1987), "The Law and Intercollegiate Athletics in Public Institutions" (Lowell 1979), *Essentials of Amateur Sports Law* (Wong 1988), and *The Law of Higher Education* (Kaplin 1985) show the legal complexities of the college athletics enterprise.

Problems in Research and Analysis

The American higher education landscape is comprised of over 2,000 institutions, and this short monograph cannot capture the nuances and details of all major institutional clusters. Instead, it focuses on the varsity sports programs at major universities—the 293 designated Division I by the National Collegiate Athletic Association as of June 1989. In some important ways, this focus tends to exempt smaller colleges from generalizations about problems in college sports. Small colleges, for example, usually do not offer athletic grants-in-aid, and because varsity sports are far from self-supporting at the 191 Division II and 313 Division III colleges, the focus here is on the self-proclaimed *revenue-producing* and *self-supporting* programs of the major universities. But a focus on Division I programs also carries a crucial codicil: Even athletics programs at small colleges have been scarred by incidents of overemphasis (Moulton 1978, pp. 13–29). Intercollegiate athletics programs at all levels face problems of rising costs. And pressures to stretch and bend rules in areas such as admissions and recruitment of student-athletes occur periodically at all intercollegiate levels, whether in the Southeastern Conference, the Ivy League, or the Little Three, Amherst, Williams, and Wesleyan.

Institutions demonstrate their priorities and commitment to philosophies in their choices about allocating resources (Lucey 1982); thus, much discussion of educational and athletics programs is grounded in the battle of the budget (Frey

1982; Miller 1982). The economics of college sports has attracted an able group of scholars whose insights are excellent, but they tend to agree that data on the topic are lacking, difficult to find, and difficult to compare. Equally frustrating as the aggregate data is the diffuse, uneven, and incomplete information from individual campuses.

> *That each institution keeps its own books in accordance with its own needs and, in the case of state institutions and community colleges, in accordance with external requirements, has not encouraged the development of reporting systems to permit sport-by-sport expenditure and income projections in light of standard definitions and universal systems for allocating overhead costs. . . . Although we collected massive amounts of information, we have no consistent data base of the sort that would permit unit cost comparison* (Atwell, Grimes, and Lopiano 1980, pp. 4–5).

For 15 years, researchers have relied on Raiborn's national reports (1974, 1978, 1986) on revenues and expenses of intercollegiate athletics programs as well as other NCAA publications for national data trends according to institutional groupings. They are approximations, however, because figures cannot be disaggregated precisely. Some of the more revealing data from the NCAA reports are not the financial totals but the context: Athletics departments are not especially forthcoming with thorough budgetary information. They are under little obligation to file, let alone publicize, uniform or detailed reports (Miller 1982; Palmer 1981, p. 66). Many institutional resources and subsidies for varsity sports can be obscured in "presidential discretionary funds" or drawn from reversions to general funds. NCAA financial data are based on limited returns (about 51 percent of member institutions), lump together Division I and Division I-AA programs, thus glossing over crucial differences among categories, and focus on program operating expenses, which are far less than "the more comprehensive expenditures" (Padilla and Boucher 1987–88). The most useful models for financial analysis are those institutional reports that compare the budgets of a particular campus program with appropriate benchmark institutions (e.g., institutions within the same conference or state), exemplified by the Washington State Council on Higher Education's report (Fischer 1975) and the comparative study of intercollegiate athletics for Montana State University and its peer campuses (Fullerton 1985).

Sensational exposes about college sports programs have become a staple in American publishing. Often they are tales out of school by former players or coaches, predictable and periodic prairie fires motivated more by an author's quest for fame than for enduring reform (Thelin 1978, pp. 179–80). This study, however, does not fit that genre: It does not rely on clandestine information or materials gained from rummaged files. To the contrary, one of the most fascinating aspects of research on college sports is the candor of and the *public* statements made by coaches and athletics directors about the scope of their programs (Bellah 1967). And the liturgy and ritual of the indictments and denials in intercollegiate sports scandals are fascinating, especially as the daily press becomes the stage for this decidedly American melodrama. Indeed, one obstacle to completing this manuscript is that virtually every day the press features yet another indictment or expose about abuses in recruiting, mismanagement of funds, law suits, or tampering with academic transcripts ad absurdum (e.g., Merritt 1985). Then suddenly the momentum shifts to celebration, usually in time for the start of a new football or basketball season. The script in large part is drafted by sports writers.

> *Anyone who deals with the sports press as well as with regular news correspondents knows how overstaffed are the sports departments of so many of our newspapers. Only a few of the major newspapers in this country even have one education writer, but the lowliest local paper has a sports staff to keep busy by overreporting the big-time programs while giving short shrift to virtually everything else.*
>
> *The media may not have created the sports-crazy society, but [they have] often spoken with forked tongue about the problem and certainly [have] not been a part of the solution. There is a hypocritical tendency on the part of some sports editorial writers to decry the scandals in big-time athletics while ignoring the plain fact that their own reporting and editorial policies have been major contributors to the problem* (Atwell 1988, p. 8).

This appraisal does not go far enough, however. A limit of many essays on reform is that they fail to ground indictments in specific cases. The following profile of a university athlete from the sports pages, with its tone of a *favorable* tribute to a star player, stands as exhibit A:

> *Steve _____ hasn't the slightest idea where he's going— unless he has a football in his hands, and then it's toward the goal line.*
>
> *"Naw, I'm just hanging around and I'm not sure what I'm going to do," the senior running back for the University of Kentucky said in an interview.*
>
> *[He] noted that he needs an extra semester to graduate after this school year and said he has no interests other than football. "Nothing interests me other than sports that I watch on TV: I play a little golf and that's it," he says* (Cooper 1975).

Significant exceptions exist, of course: Some sports editors seriously examine the topic. But misplaced praise is more the norm than the exception in daily sports journalism across the country, and first-rate analysis is usually done on special assignment by editors, reporters, and feature writers outside the sports department (see, e.g., Marx and York 1985b). Indeed, contextual analysis reinforces the finding that the "big news" is that college sports in recent years has been covered outside the sports pages, often under national news and in op-ed pieces (see, e.g., McGuff 1989).

A Framework for Institutional Evaluation

To bemoan the uneven quality of the prodigious volume of available data ultimately begs the question of critical analysis. The primary problem is identifying reasonable criteria by which to analyze the condition of college sports. Selection requires diplomacy and fairness. Coaches and athletics directors probably are wary of an audit based wholly on faculty values on the understandable grounds that professors place too much emphasis on scholarship and are out of touch with the reality and diversity of American culture, let alone the demands of administering a sports program (Blackburn and Nyikos 1974; Guttmann 1982; Miller 1982; Scott 1956). One guard against that bias is to look for standards prepared and endorsed within the world of intercollegiate athletics.

The resolution, then, is to present critical analyses of institutions and programs based on standards in the readily available guides published by the NCAA. In particular, this entire study is grounded in benchmarks drawn from appropriate sections of the NCAA's *Evaluation of Intercollegiate Athletic Programs* (1981). The rationale is that doing so diminishes the tendency for analysis to be based on criteria alien to intercollegiate sports. Using the guidelines recommended by the NCAA itself seems fair, even favorably predisposed toward having college athletics departments evaluated appropriately.

This study started as a straightforward, systematic analysis but soon became a cross between "Twilight Zone" and *Fantastic Voyage*. Intercollegiate athletics appears to have a logical place in the structure and ethos of higher education (Massengale and Merriman 1981), yet on closer inspection, varsity sports is a world turned upside down with its own peculiar logic, code, and organizational behavior (Scott 1956; Thelin 1978). To make sense of it all, the research for each chapter has three primary strands:

1. How do recent findings by social scientists and scholars in a variety of academic disciplines shape systematic thinking about college sports?
2. How do recent *events*—court cases, NCAA decisions, and institutional actions—as reported in the national press and popular media shape the structure, character, and image of college sports?
3. How might a fusion of these markedly different sources of information lead to some insights, tools, and strategies for self-study and reform of college sports by leaders and administrators? Here is where the standards suggested in the NCAA's *Evaluation of Intercollegiate Athletic Programs* is used as an analytic tool.

The aim is to provide a concise review, synthesis, and primer for college officials and leaders, including presidents, deans, board members, faculty, and alumni. For those college and university presidents, faculty, and administrators who already work closely with varsity sports, many of the themes presented will be familiar. Yet for many in higher education, the nuances of intercollegiate athletics are alien. Emphasis here is less on history and more on the conditions and events from roughly 1970 to the present. The ultimate concern is the link between intercollegiate sports and the larger sphere of educational policy and academic structure.

The authors' hypothesis in reviewing the literature is that mechanisms and codes are already in place to define and regulate the proper place of intercollegiate athletics as part of American colleges and universities. These arrangements work unevenly, however, often poorly (Frey 1982, pp. 227–29). Perhaps a major research question is whether this uneven, ineffective oversight is by accident or design.

This monograph is intended to be provocative and practical. It presents an overview of some specific proposals for reform, for example, changes in institutional mission statements, changes in regional accreditation standards, critical analysis that indicates the dysfunction of proposals calling for the national deregulation of college sports, consideration of an internal tax that would treat overhead for intercollegiate athletics programs similarly to that for federal research grants. One conspicuous item that emerges from several studies is the seemingly contradictory point that the university president should do both more and less with college sports to ensure integrity and balance (American Council on Education 1979, pp. 347–49). In matters of control, for example, separate athletics foundations could be dissolved and brought within the university structure, with the athletics director reporting directly to the academic vice president or to the vice president for business affairs. The analysis of recent research indicates that such a structure of campus governance does not put the university president into a contradictory situation; rather, it frees presidents for attention to tend to appropriate matters of leadership associated with intercollegiate sports, including collective and cooperative projects with other college and university presidents. At the same time, such structural reforms integrate intercollegiate athletics more fully into the complete fabric of campus decision making and accountability. Finally, the monograph brings attention to trends in tax law for nonprofit organizations and in practices of municipal taxation to alert colleges to the prospect of forfeiting customary protections and exemptions long afforded athletics programs affiliated with colleges.

This study does not deal much with student-athletes and the college experience. Omission is not oversight, however. Rather, the abundance of important research on the topic suggests it warrants its own comprehensive review and analysis.

The Authors' Research Perspectives

The authors bring to this study distinctive perspectives—combined academic backgrounds that include grounding in the liberal arts, biological sciences, history, educational studies, and public policy; experience as graduate students, administrators, and faculty members at major universities in both the public and private sectors; service as chair and member of a universitywide athletics policy advisory committee.

This analysis of the economic and policy dimensions of intercollegiate athletics is based on a distinctive premise: that the magnetism of intercollegiate athletics is the desire for *winning* teams. Other analysts argue that money or the pursuit of profits is the primary force driving the intercollegiate sports machinery. The authors' small but important distinction is that although winning may require money, university constituencies of fans, alumni, boosters, board members, and students foremost seek the prestige and visibility of championship teams. This focus may well engender abuses of commercialism, but it is not primarily the pursuit of financial profit that explains the prominent place spectator sports hold on the American campus.

Importantly, the authors believe in and support strong varsity sports programs (Thelin 1981; Wiseman 1986). Thus, this analysis is not a polemical diatribe or an abolitionist tract. On the other hand, the authors are neither apologists nor zealous boosters; rather, their concern is that review of the scholarly literature shows how some prominent conditions and trends in college sports, especially at the university level, are potentially destructive for both athletics and for the whole fabric of higher education. Informed discussion inside and outside the campus community could be a sorely needed starting point for rescue operations to achieve a healthy balance between academics and athletics.

FISCAL FITNESS? The Peculiar Economics of Intercollegiate Athletics

One recurrent criticism is that college sports have become a big business characterized by commercialism and professionalism, with the implicit message that reform ought be high on the agenda of colleges and universities (Frey 1982, pp. 223–38; Koch 1971; Rooney 1985; Scott 1956, pp. 29–30). "If one had to point to a single factor among the many that have corrupted college sports, it would be money" (Atwell 1988, p. 9). Reformers depict college sports as a business, as Big and Bad, and as indelibly linked to scandals and excesses. Typical of this point of view is the following editorial, which warned that "today's state of athletics is a cancer of corruption":

It is a sick, sad spectacle, and versions of it can be found on every campus where books rank second to ballgames and school officials worship the dollar instead of the Dewey Decimal System. . . . Quite simply, the world of college sports lacks a moral center. In it, goodness is not a virtue; the millions of dollars that TV lavishes on powerhouse schools are all the greedy alumni and athletic directors care about (Schulian 1985).

The "curse of bigness" is reinforced by reports of national revenues from televised tournaments and annual attendance figures. In 1981, for example, intercollegiate sports accounted for $700 million in revenues. Attendance at college football games in 1987 was over 35 million. College football television contracts now exceed $30 million per year. Such aggregate summaries confirm the magnitude of college football and basketball as spectator and broadcast activities, bringing to mind the economy of a medium-sized European country rather than an extracurricular campus activity. In 1987, sports expenditures increased 7 percent to $47.2 billion, more than 1 percent of the GNP, and ranked as the 25th largest sector of the GNP (Associated Press 1987d).

Moral outrage is not a good starting point for critical analysis, mainly because no one *denies* that college sports have become big business. In 1986, for example, the athletics director at Florida State University told a reporter, "I'm not afraid to say it: It's a business" (quoted in Goodwin 1986, p. 83; cf. McGuff 1989; Sage 1982, p. 136). Advocates of big-time college sports cite the same data on finances of intercollegiate

As a whole, American intercollegiate athletics programs are unable to support themselves. . . and most programs run a deficit.

athletics as do critics—but for a markedly different reason: to justify additional expenditures. During congressional hearings held in 1975, the athletics director of the University of Maryland told a subcommittee that his department opposed equal opportunity for women's varsity sports—"To me, this is poor business and poor management"—and noted that the university was "in competition with professional sports and other entertainment for the consumer's money" and "did not want a lesser product to market" (Asher 1975; Thelin 1978, p. 180). Similarly, a coach at another large state university explained to reporters that a losing season and bad publicity hurt his program because "We're in the entertainment business and are susceptible to the whims of fans who may get upset with our performance" (Thelin 1978, pp. 180–81).

Analysis here takes a different approach. Moral outrage in deploring college sports as a big business has yet to be an effective strategy for reforming institutional practice. And such outrage often incorrectly implies that the fall from grace is recent (Scott 1956, p. 33). In fact, practices of promoting, selling, and broadcasting college sports have roots at least to the 1920s (Hardy and Berryman 1982, pp. 15–28). If commercialism and bigness are problems, they are hardly new. It is time to stop being shocked by such indictments as though they are unprecedented or unforeseen. An alternate analysis is preferable: If, in fact, college presidents and trustees accept that Division I varsity sports are big time and largely commercial in nature (Miller 1982, pp. 92–93; Nelson 1982, pp. 52–57), what is the condition of these programs when analyzed by standards of business practice?

The Business of University Athletics: Financial Trends since 1970

A business truism is that survival depends in large part on the ability of an enterprise to generate income that exceeds expenditures. By this basic criterion, genuine albeit unexpected cause for concern about the "business health" of college sports exists at all levels (Atwell, Grimes, and Lopiano 1980, pp. 1–4; Thelin 1981). The amount of television revenues and gate receipts often conjures the image of university sports programs as money makers. It may be true but usually overlooked is that varsity programs are also money spenders. Big-time college sports as a business for colleges and universities is fragile, risky, fraught with contradictions, and run according to expectations and practices that would be suspect in the business world (Miller 1982, p. 99; Sack 1982, pp. 83–85). Furthermore, virtually every deficit in sports programs at major universities and at small colleges appears to be increasing year by year (Fischer 1975; Frey 1982, pp. 234–35; Fullerton 1985; Moulton 1978, pp. 13–29).

The first alert to problems in financing intercollegiate athletics comes from periodic reports prepared for the NCAA (Raiborn 1974, 1978, 1986). A review of the reports published over the past decade indicates that, as a whole, American intercollegiate athletics programs are unable to support themselves and that most programs run a deficit. This finding is not surprising in colleges that designate varsity sports as part of the educational budget and make no claim to seek massive crowds. It does warrant concern, however, when one looks at institutions that have established varsity football and/or basketball as major, self-supporting activities intended to produce revenues, with large arenas and stadia and with television audiences (Atwell, Grimes, and Lopiano 1980, pp. 2–4). Even within this select group, the NCAA reports indicate financial strain (Thelin 1981). The best estimate is that Division I contains big winners and big losers in "the Money Game" (Atwell, Grimes, and Lopiano 1980).

The Anatomy of an Athletics Budget: The Cases of Michigan, Kentucky, Missouri, and Maryland

One way to understand the diverse conditions of big-time sports programs is to consider selected institutional case. The aggregate data of Raiborn's NCAA studies break down NCAA institutions into large clusters, but even such groupings tend to mask substantial differences in the financial condition of institutions within each group. The aggregate NCAA data have been distilled into reasonable terms (Padilla and Boucher 1987–88): A university's varsity sports program is best depicted as the financial equivalent of a large academic department within a campus, with an annual budget of about $10 million merely for operating costs, excluding capital improvements and facilities. This size budget is probably second only to a medical school among academic units within the university scheme (Padilla and Boucher 1987–88).

Profiles of fiscal fitness in
major university sports programs

A good example of a large, well-regarded athletics program is the one at the University of Michigan. The athletics department operates as a legally separate entity, housed on what is called the "athletic campus" adjacent to the university in Ann Arbor. Its annual $15 million budget supports 130 full-time employees, including a travel agent, mechanics, carpenters, and engineers, along with several hundred part-time employees who work at games. Its facilities are valued at over $200 million and include 12 buildings, one of which is a stadium that seats over 100,000 spectators. The athletics department spent about $10 million in recent years to renovate existing facilities; annual maintenance costs are $100,000. The University of Michigan athletics department pays the university $40,000 to administer the department's payroll. The athletics director describes its self-contained character:

We cut our own grass, shovel our own snow, put on roofs, negotiate with unions. . . . We're borrowing $3 million to build a new swimming pool. The university will not be liable for that debt. We will (Canham, quoted in Goodwin 1986, p. 84).

Even this success story has an unexpected, troubling side. In September 1988, the University of Michigan athletics department announced a projected budget deficit of about $2.5 million for FY 1989, increasing to $5.2 million by 1993. The assistant athletics director reported that expenses "were likely to increase by almost 25 percent, while revenues are expected to increase by only 15 percent over the next five years" (Robert DeCarolis, quoted in Associated Press 1988b). Such developments illustrate the fragility of even established, well-supported athletics programs.

Another interesting benchmark institution in Division I-A is the University of Kentucky Athletic Association:

[The University of Kentucky's] total sports program is completely self-sustaining financially. UKAA does not receive support from the state of Kentucky or the general fund of the university. UK is unlike every other school in the state and, in fact, most schools nationally in that no tax dollars support the athletics program. Funding comes from ticket

*sales, television receipts, guarantees, and . . . contribution[s]
to the Blue and White Fund* (University of Kentucky Athletic
Association 1987).

The University of Kentucky is positioned well in the athletics
market: It belongs to the high-powered Southeastern Conference, has no nearby professional teams with which it must
compete for fans, has a relatively new, large stadium, has a
varsity basketball program with a tradition of conference and
national championships, and attracts sellout crowds in its
24,000-seat arena.

UKAA's FY 1987 operations budget of $10.6 million (which
did not include capital projects such as an indoor football
training facility, a tennis center, and a proposed stadium
expansion) included $5.5 million (51.5 percent) from sales
of football and basketball tickets, $1.3 million (12 percent)
from broadcast and television rights, and income from television rebates, guarantees, sports camps, interest, and "other."
Expenses included $2.7 million (25.6 percent) for personal
services, $1.9 million (18.1 percent) for current expenses, $1.7
million (16.6 percent) for grants-in-aid for 315 student-
athletes, and smaller amounts for guarantees, team travel,
maintenance and repairs, sports camps, game expenses,
recruiting, publicity, and medical expenses. UKAA invests
$200,000 in its program for tutoring and counseling student-
athletes. Although UKAA does not match the size and solidity
of the University of Michigan's athletics program, it is in very
healthy financial shape. In spring 1988, for example, UKAA
donated $4 million to the university's general academic pro-
grams to offset shortfalls in funding from the legislature and
other sources (Lederman 1988d).

Even the healthy UKAA is susceptible to rising costs and
fluctuating finances, however. By 1988–89, UKAA's budget
increased to $14.9 million (including $1.3 million for capital
improvements). The proposed budget for 1989–90 is $16 mil-
lion (including $1.9 million for capital improvements). Annu-
ally increasing expenditures were approved as part of the budget, even though UKAA officials projected declining revenues
for both football and basketball (Combs 1989, p. 8). UKAA's
strategy is to rely increasingly on private donations. And
although the athletics program receives no support from tax
dollars or the university's general fund, its 1988–89 revenues
included $450,000 from the university's student activities fees.

Some of the changes in UKAA's projected revenues are a result of recent NCAA investigations and penalties: legal fees, forfeiture of revenues from the 1988 NCAA basketball tournament, and, for the 1990 men's basketball season, loss of television broadcast revenues and a ban against playing in Southeastern Conference and NCAA tournaments (Combs 1989; Oberlander 1989).

For profiles of sustained financial strain, one must look beyond the University of Michigan and the University of Kentucky Athletic Association to two other major universities that compete in NCAA's Division I-A: the University of Missouri and the University of Maryland.

Profiles of big universities with big budget problems

A major program with its cumulative problems is exemplified in the University of Missouri at Columbia, with its annual budget of $6.9 million in 1979–80. Although not as successful in winning or in receipts as, for example, the University of Oklahoma or the University of Southern California, "Mizzou" is an interesting case because it is admittedly "big time," usually is among the top 10 nationwide in terms of attendance at football games, belongs to the formidable Big Eight Conference, and has the leverage of being the only Division I football team in its state. The varsity athletics program relies heavily on football to fund over 80 percent of the entire sports program; to that end, the administration, alumni, and citizens of the state have been enthusiastic supporters. The stadium was enlarged from 55,000 to 65,000 seats—and is sold out for all home games. A decade ago the Missouri football program raised $5.7 million, but it cost $3.2 million to operate the same football program, with major expenses including $375,000 for coaches' salaries, $314,000 for grants-in-aid for football players, $234,000 for travel, and $137,500 for recruiting (Gilbert 1980).

Part of the University of Missouri's income from athletics comes from revenue sharing in the Big Eight Conference. Since Gilbert's 1980 study, however, Missouri's teams have not won conference championships or played in national bowl games that would greatly increase incomes beyond annual inflationary gains, and expenses have soared far greater than revenue. Most important is that this program is *successful:* It fills all the seats in a large stadium, with no room for growth. The best option for raising additional money is through booster clubs and alumni donations.

To understand how seemingly strong athletics programs get into financial binds, consider the recent situation at the University of Maryland. Since 1985, the University of Maryland's athletics department has been struggling to maintain national-caliber play for its eight nonrevenue varsity men's sports, along with its primary commitment to football and basketball. Declining resources and reductions in grants-in-aid are the explanations given for deteriorating won-loss records in such sports as track, lacrosse, wrestling, baseball, and swimming. But even the sports expected to produce revenues have a long record of falling short. The football program lost $300,000 to $400,000 every year from 1978 to 1981 (Jenkins 1985), and by 1987, the intercollegiate athletics department had a deficit of over $1 million, eventually leading the athletics director to fire 17 employees in the ticket office, marketing, public relations, training, and maintenance (Jenkins 1987a). Why did the department fail to balance its $8.3 million annual budget? First, football gate receipts fell $600,000 below projections. Second, the University of Maryland lost $350,000 when the Cherry Bowl could not pay its guaranteed money after the Terrapins appeared in the postseason football game in 1985. Third, basketball showed a deficit of $150,000. And finally, "former basketball coach Lefty Driesell was guaranteed $136,000 a year for the next eight years when he was forced to resign . . . and become an assistant athletic director. . . . " Further, the athletics director who resigned was paid $77,000 for one year as a consultant (Jenkins 1987b). By 1989, the Maryland athletics program projected an annual deficit of about $200,000 and was proposing to ask the state legislature to consider a direct subsidy to intercollegiate athletics (Sell and Goldstein 1989). In summer 1989, the department's expenses increased again, when the University of Maryland athletics department carried *another* former varsity men's basketball coach on its payroll and hired a new basketball coach for an estimated base annual salary of $100,000 (Asher 1989).

The cases of Missouri and Maryland are especially disconcerting because both are large public flagship universities that enjoy support from the administration and alumni, neither faces competition from another Division I university within the state, and each has a large football stadium and basketball arena. Both are in good locations for attendance and both enjoy widespread coverage by the media. The conferences to which they belong (the Big Eight and the Atlantic Coast Conference, respectively) profit from good television contracts and have revenue-sharing programs for all conference members. They are big-time programs operating with blessings and advantages, yet both illustrate how the alleged revenue-producing sports are susceptible to consuming rather than generating operating funds. And the precarious finances of Maryland and Missouri are not isolated (see, e.g., Fischer 1975). Nearly 10 years ago at the University of Colorado, the athletics director told reporters that the department was "almost broke," leading one journalist to conclude, "College football has a case of the shorts" (Moss 1981).

Response to financial pressure at a number of large universities has been to cut nonrevenue varsity sports or to adopt a policy of "tiering," in which the athletics department makes conscious decisions to target some non-revenue-producing sports for reduced funding, limited facilities, few athletic scholarships, and local schedules. At the University of Washington in 1974–75, the board of regents considered a proposal to eliminate athletic grants-in-aid for all varsity sports except men's football and men's and women's basketball (Fischer 1975, p. 6). The board rejected the proposal, opting instead to attempt to maintain grants-in-aids for student-athletes in all varsity sports. That solution was unaffordable, however, and led the University of Washington to drop two varsity sports—wrestling and men's gymnastics—in which it had enjoyed national prominence.

The most novel contribution to policy discussion to come from the state of Washington's council on higher education is its focus on the expenses rather than the income associated with operating college sports programs; that is, the report prompts colleges and universities to abandon the notion of categorizing sports as "revenue producing" and to increase emphasis on whether or not a given sport is "revenue consuming" (Fischer 1975). The Washington report counters the customary response of athletics department officials to meet the problem of growing expenses by favoring increased revenues (Palmer 1981, p. 66).

An example of financial reform through reducing the sports program comes from the Southeastern Conference (SEC). By 1979:

> . . . inflation and the cost of adding sports to the program
> were major concerns among Southeastern Conference ath-

letics directors. Athletics administrators endorsed more plans to increase revenues than reduce expenditures. The majority of the directors favored abolishing scholarships in non-revenue sports, while the major thrust for increased revenues was in the area of contributions and donations (Nader 1982, pp. xi–xii).

For example, varsity wrestling was added as a championship sport in the SEC in the 1970s and quickly gained national stature. Despite nationally ranked teams, wrestling has since been dropped at Louisiana State University, the University of Kentucky, and the University of Tennessee. Similarly, outside the SEC, the University of Colorado eliminated varsity baseball, wrestling, and swimming. Oregon State University recently announced it was cutting funding for varsity track and cross country, even though those sports have a tradition of conference and national championships (Moore 1988). The College of William and Mary cut several varsity sports and Stanford reduced funding for nine of its intercollegiate teams in 1984. One cost-cutting measure is to change the format of competition; dual track meets have virtually disappeared, for example, in favor of multiteam invitational meets. A problem of the strategy of reduction, however, is that it undermines a fundamental justification for big-time football and basketball: prime providers for educationally balanced, diverse athletics programs. In fact, big-time football is often not a means to a comprehensive program; in lean times, it is an end in itself—and often unable even to support itself (Lopiano 1979).

Why Are Expenses for College Sports So High?

Expenses for big-time sports tend to rise substantially more than annual inflationary rates, in part because athletics departments ascribe to expensive customs. In some states, for example, athletics administrators at public universities have justified requests for direct state appropriations to varsity sports on the grounds that "it takes money to make money," implying that the state legislature should provide initial resources for starting an athletics fund-raising program (Palmer 1981, p. 73). Second is the traditional belief that "a happy athlete is a winning athlete" (Sack 1982; Stump 1976). Conspicuous consumption for student-athletes often is standard practice, suggested, for example, by construction of special dormitories.

In 1974, the University of Pittsburgh's athletics officials proudly told *Time* magazine that their football program included $600,000 for operating the program, $350,000 for scholarships (140 players at $2,500 each), and $30,000 for the head coach's salary. Donations of $181,000 from alumni over two years went for enlarging locker rooms and installing carpeting, a lounge, and a stereo system. The coach noted, "Carpeting floors doesn't win ball games for you, but it sure makes things more comfortable" (*Time* 1974). Another enduring custom of big-time college sports is faith in certain activities as necessary for achieving a winning team in a revenue-producing sport. Most Division I football coaches, for example, have the entire squad and staff spend Friday night at a local hotel, even before a home game (Heyman 1987a).

College coaches are not especially precise in their ability to select talented student-athletes. Division I-A football squads are allowed to have 95 athletes receiving full grants-in-aid, a number sufficient to subsidize more than four players at each of the 22 slots constituting a complete starting lineup. Reliance on such an inordinate number of scholarship players usually represents a coach's hedge against several problems: high attrition as a result of scholastic ineligibility, athletes' failure to play to their predicted potential, and "stockpiling" outstanding athletes to prevent opposing teams from having access to their talent. All three practices are expensive and wasteful (Guttmann 1982, pp. 74–75; Rooney 1987).

Attempts at frugality and reduction are uneven. Athletics directors and football coaches have been reluctant to endorse compacts that would promote significant savings in athletic grants-in-aid, leading to what has been called the "athletics arms race" (Heyman 1987a). Under current guidelines, a Division I-A team may provide 95 football grants-in-aid in a given year, Division I-AA 70 (NCAA 1989, Article 15.5). Proposals to reduce numbers in either category have been defeated at recent NCAA annual meetings. Most disconcerting is that athletic grants-in-aid do not have to be based on a student-athlete's showing financial need (Lowell 1979; NCAA 1982, pp. 1–16).

Another expensive practice is that universities pay high salaries to selected coaches. At several major universities, the head football or basketball coach makes over $100,000 in annual base salary, sometimes more than the university president. And, as exemplified earlier in the discussion about the

University of Maryland, big-time athletics departments follow the custom of buying up multiyear contracts for a fired coach. The University of North Carolina at Chapel Hill, for example, regarded as having a well-run, model, big-time program, is reported to have "bought up" a fired football coach's contract for over $800,000 (Oberlander 1988b).

College Sports and Life without Television: The Economics of Division I-AA Programs

For the relatively few Division I universities whose football and basketball teams enjoy television coverage, luxuries are affordable and can exist within the bounds of a balanced budget. This style becomes harder to maintain, however, among less visible programs in Division I-A and is especially hard to maintain in Division I-AA. Most of this monograph has dealt with Division I programs because they are likely to claim the ability and responsibility to be both self-supporting and revenue producing, exclusive of such subsidies as mandatory student fees. This literature review has not included much about sports programs at small colleges because most such institutions have no mandate to be self-supporting, auxiliary enterprises, let alone money makers (Fischer 1975, pp. 43–52). Where one places the varsity sports program within the institution determines in large measure the kinds of financial questions one uses to evaluate the program (Moulton 1978). The NCAA's data do suggest that college programs in Divisions II and III are experiencing rising costs—and that the gap between expenses and revenues is increasing dramatically. Sports programs at small colleges function without athletic grants-in-aid and without the expectation that sports contests will bring in substantial revenues, but this lack can work only if the varsity sports program is truly defined and funded as part of the immediate educational experience (Lucey 1982) or as a genuine part of student services, with participation in varsity sports open to all students (Fischer 1975, pp. 2–3). In dramatic contrast to the Division I institutions' quest for broadcast publicity, the highly successful football coach at Amherst College (Division III) rejected the opportunity to have the traditional Little Three Game against Williams College televised because he thought the broadcast and camera crews would intrude on the character and quality of the campus and the game (Carlson 1985).

Below the Mount Olympus of the Big Eight, the Big Ten,

The Ivy League stands as a significant, successful model in which a group of eight institutions have integrated high academic standards with Division I athletics.

the Atlantic Coast, the Pacific Ten, the Southwestern, and the Southeastern conferences, the financial condition of Division I-AA is interesting and important for understanding the increasing strains and dilemmas of financing highly competitive varsity sports. Division I-AA includes the Ivy League institutions (Brown, Columbia, Cornell, Dartmouth, Harvard, Pennsylvania, Princeton, and Yale—where football teams are *not* expected to be self-supporting), many major state universities (e.g., the Yankee Conference with the universities of Massachusetts, Connecticut, Delaware, Rhode Island, Vermont, Maine, and New Hampshire), and the privately endowed University of Richmond. Their scope and attendance were deemed too small by the major powers—and hence were relegated to a separate cluster within the NCAA in 1981. A typical Division I-AA team's stadium seats only 15,000 to 30,000, and data suggest the difficulty revenue-producing sports have being self-sufficient in the 1980s. One survey of 16 prominent Division I-AA football programs showed that 15 reported substantial deficits in 1987 (the 16th institution refused to respond to the survey) (Radford 1987). The three Division I-AA football programs in Virginia face severe financial problems (Lipper 1987). For the 1986 season, for example, the football team at James Madison University had expenses of slightly over $1 million and revenues from ticket sales, concessions, and guarantees of $143,054—a deficit of almost $900,000; for 1984, 1985, and 1986 combined, James Madison's football program lost more than $2.3 million, William and Mary's $2.4 million, and Virginia Military Institute's $1.9 million (Lipper 1987). (Deficits usually were covered by funds from mandatory student fees.) Ironically, they are considered to be among the healthiest, best-supported Division I-AA football programs in terms of alumni interest and attendance.

Among Division I-AA *public* institutions, the tendency is for athletics directors and coaches to justify funds for athletic grants-in-aid and use of student fees for varsity sports on the grounds that a public institution cannot be expected to compete with Ivy League schools and other well-endowed private colleges that allegedly can offer their students generous financial aid. The argument that the Ivy League enjoys a significant advantage in attracting top student-athletes, however, tends to gloss over the view that the Ivy League institutions' commitment to distinctive educational principles means that their varsity sports programs "face unique limitations" in attracting student-athletes. The Ivy League, for example, prohibits athletic grants-in-aid and requires adherence to selective academic admissions and financial aid based on students' need. Above all, "conference guidelines suggest that athletes, as a group, must be similar to the entire student body in terms of past academic performance" (Associated Press 1987b; cf. Atwell, Grimes, and Lopiano 1980, pp. 14–16; Lederman 1986).

The Ivy League stands as a significant, successful model in which a group of eight institutions have integrated high academic standards with Division I athletics in a large number of sports for both men and women. Although the Ivy institutions are financially well-endowed, the conference is not without its own problems. For example, "The eight Ivy League schools are a special case not only because of their prestige, but also because they present some interesting problems that go beyond the few institutions involved. . . . Recruiting is very intense; in some sports at some institutions, the pressure to win compares with that of high-intensity programs in major athletic powers that award grants-in-aid to athletes" (Atwell, Grimes, and Lopiano 1980, p. 14). According to a press account, "The economic realities of an Ivy education don't bode well for the leaguewide improvement in the near future" (Associated Press 1987b). In 1987, the football coach at Columbia commented, "Money, in the last 10 or 15 years, has become the biggest obstacle that's faced" the Ivy League (Larry McElreavy, quoted in Associated Press 1987b). This view is reinforced in a comment about the contemporary situation in the Ivy League:

> *If Ivy schools are not attracting as many outstanding athletes, it is not because they do not want them. In addition to the fact that academic standards remain high, there is one problem that is more serious than ever—finances. Rising costs have hit hard at the middle class, perhaps the best source of tough, motivated athletes. In the mid-1970s the cost of attending an Ivy League school was less than $6,000 annually, and when a partial financial aid package fell short of the needed amount, loans were available at interest rates of 3 percent.*
>
> *Ten years later, the cost is over $15,000, loans are more difficult to obtain, and more than a few Ivy coaches are losing prized recruits for one reason only: They can't afford*

to turn down athletic scholarships from outside the league
(Bertagna 1986, p. 3).

The result is a classic rivalry within Division I-AA in which
both sides—coaches at public and at private institutions—
depict each other as having an advantage in recruiting student-
athletes. Hence, athletics directors and coaches urge their own
institution and prospective alumni donors to provide more
resources to remain competitive with rival teams. "Keeping
up with the varsity Joneses" provides one rationale for
increased athletic fund raising. It sometimes also provides
a case for escalating resources that go directly or indirectly
to athletics programs; in the Ivy League, for example, the football coach at the University of Pennsylvania advocated "pref-
erential packaging" for football players "in which they would
get their full need in a grant rather than a package that also
obligates them to work and take a loan that must be repaid"
(Ed Zubrow, quoted in Associated Press 1987b). And, as suggested in the discussion of Division I-AA public institutions,
the argument for more resources takes place even in those
athletics programs that already show substantial annual
deficits.

Philanthropy and Fund Raising

The most popular solution athletics departments use to close
the gap between flat revenues of ticket sales and rising
expenses is to solicit donations (Frey 1982, pp. 229–30). Some
evidence suggests that even among the major conferences,
private contributions still surpass television revenues as the
mainstay of institutional athletic resources. Data from the
Atlantic Coast Conference (ACC) in the early 1980s supports
this view. For 1981–82, the eight private fund-raising organizations of the ACC member universities raised $15 million.
The usual mechanism for such activity is through booster
clubs and "athletics/educational foundations" (Alberger
1981). Clemson's IPTAY Club ("I Pay Thirty A Year Club")
raised $3.16 million in one year, followed by Chapel Hill's
Ram's Club ($2.6 million), and North Carolina State's Wolfpack
Club and Virginia's Booster Club ($2 million each). Georgia
Tech was lowest in the conference at $1 million (United Press
International 1982).

The $15 million raised by ACC members does not include
special fund-raising campaigns: In one 18-month period, the

University of North Carolina raised $22 million for its new basketball arena, Georgia Tech raised $6.7 million for a new sports complex, and Duke University received $3 million in special gifts for new sports facilities. The universities that belong to the Southeastern Conference are similarly successful in fund raising. Although it was noted that the University of Kentucky's Athletic Association is a "strong" fund-raising program, UKAA's literature in 1987 reminded prospective donors that it was still a "poor cousin" among its benchmark institutions: "The University of Kentucky currently ranks near the bottom of the Southeastern Conference in the amount of money raised for athletics. While other schools are raising in the $2 to $4 million . . . range, contributions to UKAA last year were less than $1 million" (University of Kentucky Athletic Association 1987).

Establishing a distinct sports foundation (usually as a corporation within or connected to the university) is a practice pursued among the Division I-A institutions, the Division I-AA Ivy League schools, and even some colleges in Divisions II and III (Barnes, Rice, and Sturrock 1981, p. 12; Frey 1982, pp. 223–38). A pivotal question is how a distinct program to raise money for college sports teams coexists with raising funds for other university activities. One view is that money raised for the university, even if earmarked for a specific program, benefits the entire institution because it frees up another university dollar to be used by the president and dean as part of total institutional planning. A brochure from the Brown University Sports Foundation (1987) illustrates this approach: "Give to the Brown Sports Foundation and you're not just giving to sports!" The explanation given is that every dollar in contributions to the sports foundation benefits "every area of the University from its scholarship fund to its library acquisition budget. Because every dollar we don't have to spend on athletics helps us fund other aspects of the Brown experience. Which means your donation not only makes you a part of Brown's athletic achievements—it makes you a part of Brown's academic success."

How in this case does the sports foundation interact with the overall institutional budget? "In the Ivy League, as in the liberal arts colleges, athletics is not expected to be self-supporting and typically is subject to the same budgetary review and constraints as other programs" (Atwell, Grimes, and Lopiano 1980, p. 15). Further, "despite a potentially gen-

erous group of 'old grads' available for booster clubs, the typical Ivy League institution prohibits or severely limits fund raising for athletic programs" (p. 15). According to a 1988 brochure, "The Brown Sports Foundation Endowment, presently $3,900,000, earns money [that] provides the University with budget relief for its sports expenditures and over $1,000,000 since its inception in 1983. The University is able to use these relief funds in support of its regular academic, counseling, and administrative programs." It is an intriguing model because it has potential to integrate budgets for athletics and academics. Yet it still raises important questions for comprehensive university planning and allocation of resources. For example, it is not evident that Brown's model necessarily keeps a lid on intercollegiate sports expenses because elsewhere in the same brochure donors are advised that the sports foundation also raises money to help programs beyond what regular university budgeted amounts provide. Another critical question connected to this model of athletics as part of total institutional planning is whether evidence or guarantee of reciprocity exists among internal constituencies; one wonders whether the history department, for example, has a fundraising brochure that makes the same point about how donations to *its* program make a donor part of Brown's athletic success.

The model illustrated by Brown University assumes integration of athletic and educational budgets (Frey 1982, p. 226). Although this situation may hold for Brown and the Ivy League institutions, many large universities (especially public institutions) have adopted a markedly different arrangement: They may be quite decentralized, with each unit discrete in its budgeting and fund raising. Such a financial structure indicates that the monies raised by a semiautonomous private corporation (as are most athletics foundations) do not enter into a single, universitywide pot. Furthermore, the idea of "sharing" dollars is unlikely in most Division I-A institutions, as most university athletics departments spend all that they raise (Frey 1982, p. 226; Lopiano 1979). And although athletics foundation directors informally emphasize cooperation with a university's other fund-raising offices (Miller 1981, p. 51), the degree of coordination historically has varied greatly from institution to institution.

If this example illustrates the notion of sports fund raising as partner with campuswide donations, interesting to consider is a more aggressive case for college sports: the notion of a multiplier effect in athletics as part of the university's total philanthropy and prestige. One proposition is that alumni contributions to college sports actually enhance academic opportunities and image, which can be so because dollar contributions that lead to winning teams accomplish two things: first, they enhance morale among a present generation of students (who will then become future loyal donors); and second, winning teams generate favorable imagery and publicity for the institution, in turn attracting more donations. This view is set forth by two Clemson University economists (McCormack and Tinsley 1987; cf. Clark 1986), who contend that their own institution has shown an increase in SAT scores among all entering students during those years when Clemson had championship sports teams. In sum, the academic side of the university benefits from visible, winning teams, because "advertising attracts more applications, giving the university a larger pool to choose from."

The two economists acknowledge some limits of this argument, however, because their conclusion is based on numerous other associations in the jump from winning teams to acquiring better students. They see higher faculty salaries, larger libraries, smaller classes, and higher endowments as part of the chain originating with contributions to athletics (Lederman 1988b). Furthermore, this argument does not speak to another syndrome: that the scandals often associated with building big-time winning teams might detract from the institution's reputation or that, even without scandal, winning teams might promote the image of a university whose first priorities are football or basketball (Thelin 1978, p. 181). The puzzle for researchers is thus whether support of athletics becomes an end in itself, or whether it becomes a source of institutional pride that also generates support to promote academic stature. The evasive nature of this question is suggested by a justification for starting a booster club by one athletics fund raiser who had worked at Clemson:

At Clemson, we had a slogan stating that IPTAY was unmistakably the very best. People at Clemson firmly believed that. They built that program on pride because of the things they've been able to accomplish through the years. Clemson is a small school in a rural part of South Carolina and really didn't have a lot to cheer about other than the fact that its

athletic teams have been doing great through the years.
Clemson raised $2.7 million last year from more than
15,000 people. These people are giving to that program
because of pride (Bennett 1981, p. 3).

How widely can one extend the study at Clemson that indicates funding for athletics benefits the institution's overall stature? Research by several other scholars suggests it extends in a limited manner. Suppose one claims that a big-time sports program boosts a university's overall *academic* reputation and resources. If it were true, one might expect a strong correlation between universities with outstanding sports programs that win national championships and membership in such prestigious academic and research organizations as the Association of American Universities. In fact, no clear connection or indication of overlap exists, for big-time athletics can at some point be incidental—or possibly contrary—to an institution's overall stature (Thelin 1978, p. 181). A study by two political scientists, "Win One for the Giver" (Sigelman and Carter 1979), systematically analyzes alumni giving and big-time sports, questioning the conventional wisdom. Their approach was to analyze institution-by-institution fund-raising data and athletic records of 138 colleges and universities that offered Division I football programs during academic year 1975–76. Contrary to anecdotal evidence, their statistical tests led them to conclude (even while recognizing the limits of systematic research on institutional practices):

We could find no support in our data for the notion that alumni giving rises and falls with the fortunes of big-time intercollegiate athletic programs. . . . Even if there were a strong relationship between athletic success and alumni giving, [it] would probably be of little practical consequence, because most schools obtain only a small portion of their support from alumni. . . . In any event, our statistical analysis has revealed that there is simply no relationship between success or failure in football and basketball and increases and decreases in alumni giving. . . . In the final analysis, however, the lack of any relationship between success in intercollegiate athletics and increased alumni giving probably matters a good deal less than the fact that so many people believe that such a relationship exists. Debates concerning the role of college sports tend rapidly to turn into ideological confrontations. . . . Because the idea can be debated so nicely from a variety of ideological outlooks, it will doubtless continue to be widely held despite the contrary evidence presented here (Sigelman and Carter 1979, pp. 291–93).

Another perspective on the connections between university fund raising and varsity sports comes from the director of information services at Notre Dame:

The common mistake of assuming a causal relationship between fund-raising success and athletic victories needs correction.

In Notre Dame's case, football was historically important in establishing national visibility for the institution, and there are undoubtedly donors whose first attraction to the university was through its athletic charisma. However, since Notre Dame established a formal fund-raising endeavor in 1946, there has been no discernible correlation between the level of giving to the university and intercollegiate athletic records. Indeed, the university's first successful capital gifts campaign took place during a 14–25 football nadir.

A recent survey of alumni motivation showed that preservation of the university's Catholic character, independent status, and academic excellence ranked far above endorsement of its sports achievements (Conklin 1978).

The case of the University of North Carolina at Chapel Hill illustrates the charge that athletic fund raising can be at odds with educational resources and prestige. Some faculty at Chapel Hill recently have argued that potent athletic fund raising has led to an overemphasis on sports, especially construction of sports facilities. At the same time the athletics department's Athletic Educational Foundation conducted its successful two-year drive for $22 million to build the new basketball arena, the university's faculty salaries were frozen in response to low state tax revenues and widespread recession. The chancellor responded to faculty members' complaints about misplaced priorities by insisting that "the center was not a priority of the university. It was a priority of the educational foundation." Although the chancellor's statement might exonerate his own office from emphasizing expenditures for athletics to the neglect of educational matters, at the very least it implies that athletics/educational foundations can and do set priorities distinct from universitywide administration and apart from the institution's primary academic mission (Lederman 1988c; Oberlander 1988b).

Research leads both scholars and fund raisers to be cautious about claims that winning varsity teams stimulate alumni contributions to the university (Sigelman and Carter 1979). While researchers generally agree that favorable publicity about sports increases a university's visibility, how it directly influences university fund raising remains unclear. "The mistake is believing that you're going to necessarily convert a strong athletic booster into an academic supporter" (Frey, quoted in Lederman 1988b; cf. Frey 1982, p. 119).

Research Strategies:
Institutional Budget Analysis

Most of the cases cited in this section deal with major athletics programs. The expenses of operating an athletics program and its affiliated foundation sometimes may be 30 percent of revenues, but institutions vary widely (Barnes, Rice, and Sturrock 1981, p. 18). A highly successful booster club at a large state university reports, for example, that "the costs of raising money are roughly 16 percent" (Miller 1981, p. 52). The cost-benefit ratio of private fund-raising organizations diminishes at institutions with low visibility, small stadia, and relatively few alumni, and monitoring the expense of fund raising is crucial. The expenses of salaries for an athletics director, a fund raiser and staff, mailings, and publicity are high. For example, the 1988–89 intercollegiate athletics budget at the University of Maryland was $8.5 million, of which about $4 million was devoted to "administrative, business, training, academic support, marketing, and golf course costs" (Sell and Goldstein 1989). Furthermore, athletics/educational foundations face increasing questions about whether they duplicate efforts and expenses of other campus fund-raising activities. Indeed, one suggestion for structural reform is that athletics/educational foundations should be increasingly under the purview of the university's vice president for university relations and the universitywide development office (Barnes, Rice, and Sturrock 1981, p. 12).

The track of where money comes from and where it goes in varsity sports programs is not readily evident. Among Florida's public colleges and universities, for example, as late as

1981 budgets for intercollegiate athletics programs were not accessible to the public. Only when athletics departments ventured into lobbying state legislators for state appropriations were "college presidents and athletics directors . . . willing to let their budgets be in the sunshine for the first time in history" (Palmer 1981, p. 65). Further, reports by athletics fund raisers tend to emphasize how much money they raise, with little information on how much they spend on the efforts (Alberger 1981; Barnes, Rice, and Sturrock 1981). Systematic analysis and comparison of expenditures for athletics programs and fund raising face the problem that until recently, athletics officials "did not know how to measure their own condition" (Palmer 1981, p. 66). One might ask the following questions in analyzing an institution's budget for athletics:

Athletics/ educational foundations can and do set priorities distinct from universitywide administration and apart from the institution's primary academic mission.

- Do varsity coaches hold faculty appointments? If so, the state funds them in part, and such salaries are not usually reported in the budget for intercollegiate athletics.
- Conversely, does the booster club raise money for coaching salaries? If so, who determines the amount of those salaries? (Miller 1981, p. 55).
- Are student fees actually reported? (Fullerton 1985, pp. 14–16).
- Who pays for grounds keeping and maintenance? (Fischer 1975).
- Are "in-kind" items (helmets, shoes, livestock for the training table) reported as revenues or as expenditures? (Bennett 1981, pp. 8–9).
- Are revenues from nonconference television broadcasts reported?
- How much in reserve does the athletics foundation hold?
- Where are salaries of employees of the athletics foundation reported? (In most states, employees' salaries at public universities are published as part of the public record, but the record often excludes those paid out of private funds, such as coaches.)
- Do athletes get free housing?
- Does the intercollegiate athletics department pay indirect overhead for use of university services for payroll, personnel, and accounting? (Miller 1981, pp. 51–55).
- Are coaches' perks in the budget? (Bennett 1981, p. 9).
- Are all direct support monies reported in public statements (e.g., funds from the president's discretionary account)?

- What are the costs and benefits of the private athletics fund-raising corporation? What is the ratio of actual funds raised for sports teams versus expenses for overhead and salaries? How does this ratio comply with standards set for the university's development offices? (Miller 1979). Does a professional organization like the Association of Governing Boards of Universities and Colleges (Oliva 1989, pp. 25–27) or the Council for Advancement and Support of Education (CASE) have performance criteria? This last question is important because athletics foundations have a tendency to proliferate in size; as the assistant executive director of Florida State University's Seminole Boosters Club reported, "We started out with an office in a one-bedroom apartment with a staff consisting of an executive director and a secretary. Now we have a two-story building and a full-time staff of 12" (Barnes, Rice, and Sturrock 1981, p. 12).
- Have incidents of slush funds and improper monies occurred? If so, how and where were such funds collected, stored, and distributed? (Hanford 1979, p. 357).

Having collected information about one's own athletics program, the next step is to compare and contrast it with practices elsewhere. To assist in this analysis, the NCAA published *Financial Reporting and Control for Intercollegiate Athletics* (1974), which presents both a survey of and recommended practices for financial reporting from NCAA member institutions. It was a voluntary survey, however, to which only 42 percent of member institutions replied, and it is limited in its ability to delineate normative behavior among college athletics programs.

Evaluating the Finances of Athletics Programs: Guidelines for Official Academic Policy and Accreditation Standards

How can one make sense of these financial and economic data in terms of the institution's total educational mission? One reasonable approach is to use the criteria recommended by the NCAA (1981), which include some guidelines on the finances of intercollegiate athletics culled from various regional accreditation handbooks. It is a good start:

The intercollegiate athletics program ought neither engross
an undue proportion of the institution's financial resources
nor contribute disproportionately to them. Its cost should
be relative to its educational significance.

All expenditures for and income from athletics, from
whatever source, should be controlled by the institution and
included in its regular accounting and budgeting
procedures.

Funds used to support all athletic programs shall be fully
controlled by the administration and shall be reflected in
an annual audit of the institution's financial records
(NCAA 1981, pp. 14–15).

One obvious strategy for reform to make intercollegiate
athletics accountable to the university's budgeting and financial planning is to make athletics part of the regular structure
for educational funding, eligible for institutional resources
along with other educational activities. To do so, however,
faces two obstacles for institutions with Division I programs.
First, in many states, the legislature—not the university administration or faculty—has determined that public institutions'
intercollegiate athletic programs (especially those with athletic
grants-in-aid) are not defined as part of the educational program eligible for regular state appropriations. Second, the
NCAA'S own philosophy statement recommends that *by definition* Division I programs ought to strive to be financed
from revenues generated by the program itself and that Division I-A football and basketball programs are *by definition*
spectator-oriented, income-producing activities (NCAA 1989,
p. 282). The case of public universities in the state of Washington suggests an interesting model for reform that addresses
these points and is congruent with the guidelines for
accreditation.

Washington's council on higher education analyzed the
financing of intercollegiate athletics in the state's universities
and recommended that each institution choose in defining
its various sports as either dependent on recruiting and athletic grants-in-aid or not. Those sports that opted for reliance
on grants-in-aid were then required to be self-sustaining.
Sports whose participants were drawn from the student body
without explicit recruitment or athletic financial awards, however, were eligible for state-appropriated funding through general expenses and administration for student services (Fischer

1975, pp. 2–3, 19–27).

The Washington proposal requires substantial internal re-definition of athletics scholarships and students' participation that may be problematic at Division I universities seeking national championship–caliber teams. Compliance with the letter and spirit of these criteria sometimes tends to conflict with existing practices for Division I athletics programs at many large universities, because few intercollegiate athletics programs would be able to justify their financial resources in terms of *educational* significance (Sack 1982; Scott 1956; Thelin 1978). Furthermore, most incorporated athletics/educational foundations are beyond thorough, direct control by the university's central administration.

If athletics departments are reluctant to ascribe to these recommended educational standards, how might current practices be made more honest and consistent with the total institutional arrangement and the NCAA's own philosophy statement for Division I? One extreme proposal that surfaces from time to time is a laissez-faire arrangement in which universities are not externally constrained in developing big-time varsity sports programs. Thus, instead of reshaping intercollegiate programs to fit existing accreditation standards, a more realistic approach might be to draft new institutional accreditation standards that reflect the actual behavior and character of intercollegiate sports programs at Division I institutions. Central to this perspective is the notion of institutional autonomy—a university has the right to operate an intercollegiate athletics program that is "commercial" or "professional" in character—which leads to the intriguing prospect of deregulation, in which the financial condition of intercollegiate programs exists in a truly self-determining open marketplace (Lawrence 1987b; Rooney 1987).

According to this arrangement, college sports would function truly as a laissez-faire "business." It is a proposal advanced by some superb analysts of intercollegiate athletics, including a geographer (Rooney 1985, 1987), political scientists (Hart-Nibbrig and Cottingham 1986), and an economist (Lawrence 1987b), each of whom concluded that many individual colleges would do well to come clean by admitting that their programs are "professional." In a similar vein, each year the Nebraska legislature considers (and rejects) a bill that would allow the university to pay salaries to varsity athletes. The gain for the university is that it drops the pretense of "athletes as students," of spectator sports as an "educational activity" or a "student extracurricular activity" misleadingly coupled with intramural and student-life programs. Under a revised code, intercollegiate athletics could be defined as a wholly distinct, auxiliary enterprise.

This proposal is attractive to some reformers because it is honest and consistent, legitimizing practices already associated with some big-time programs, and because commercialism and professionalism are inevitable among major college teams, why not allow such practices? An important caveat, however, is that most universities, even those with big-time varsity athletics programs, would *not* be well served by this proposal. Few universities could be serious about establishing a truly professional sports program. For all the publicity about the prominence of varsity teams at Oklahoma, Kentucky, and other universities, even within the 66-member Central Football Association, most Division I athletics programs could not survive as truly professional or commercial ventures (Frey 1982, pp. 234–35). Certainly Division I-AA institutions, already troubled with limited revenues and few prospects for television audiences, would fail as "professional" enterprises. And it is useful to keep in mind the attrition of professional athletic leagues: The World Football League and the United States Football League have gone bankrupt in the last decade. Even the New England Patriots of the established National Football League has had trouble meeting the players' payroll during the past two years. Professional sports often are a notoriously risky enterprise and would be a disastrous financial model for most university athletics departments.

Some do not go so far as to compare big-time college sports to a "professional model" (Atwell, Grimes, and Lopiano 1980), opting instead for the term "semiprofessional." This distinction is good and important. Despite large crowds, television audiences, concessions, souvenirs to sell, and so on, only a handful of college football or basketball teams could truly support themselves as a "business enterprise"—and an even smaller number of intercollegiate athletics departments with a range of sports beyond football and/or basketball could bring in sufficient revenues to be healthy. A more accurate description is to acknowledge that intercollegiate athletics at all levels are at least partly subsidized by the institution. And cumulative NCAA activities are probably best characterized as a cartel, not a free-market industry (Lawrence 1987b).

Whether or not deregulation is workable, major intercollegiate athletics programs increasingly will face the syndrome of "the rich get richer." A handful of institutions that enjoy television coverage and winning teams skew the data and imagery of college sports as a lucrative venture. A better estimate is that in all cases it is an *expensive* venture characterized by substantial initial and hidden costs whose profits are highly risky. The growing imbalance between prosperous and poor athletics programs can be addressed by adopting some level of revenue sharing (Weistart 1987, pp. 15–16). If implemented by the NCAA, revenue sharing might promote survival of several conferences and institutional programs. Although some conferences already follow this practice, its limit is that it may help the wealthier conferences but exclude financially weaker leagues and large numbers of independent institutions.

Rather than describe major college sports as big businesses, it is more accurate to see them as large indulgences. An apt metaphor for big-time college sports is that of a huge animal whose spurts of energy are accompanied by a voracious appetite in an environment that is running out of resources (Thelin 1981, pp. 39–41). Even though in many institutions, especially public universities, college sports are expected by law to be self-supporting, auxiliary enterprises, most programs have trouble fulfilling this charge. As of 1981, for example, "the state of Florida [did] not give any money for the support of athletic programs or for the expansion of athletic facilities" (Barnes, Rice, and Sturrock 1981, p. 13), yet in that same year, athletics officials at Florida's public institutions initiated lobbying that led to direct and indirect state appropriations for women's intercollegiate athletics to "stabilize" varsity programs (Palmer 1981, p. 73). In sum, the beast cannot adequately feed itself. Big-time college sports is a *subsidized* activity that is allowed to survive and grow for various reasons quite apart from the ability to generate direct revenues.

One problem of analysis and reform is confusion over definitions. In 1988, the State Higher Education Executive Officers (SHEEO) analyzed a survey of policies and practices on the funding of intercollegiate athletics in 13 states and included a cautionary note from the National Association of College and University Business Officers:

Intercollegiate athletics often present a problem in classification. Some are operated for the entertainment of the public as well as for student participation, while others are conducted solely for student participation. If the operation is largely self-supporting, it is logical and appropriate to classify it as an auxiliary enterprise. When the athletic program is intended primarily for student participation, intercollegiate athletics, along with intramurals, may be classified as an educational and general activity (SHEEO 1988).

The working definition in this monograph is that a *self-supporting* intercollegiate program is one that raises its own resources (from donors, gate receipts, broadcast rights, and so on), with production intended to surpass consumption. By this standard, a program that seeks substantial revenues from ticket sales and donors yet relies regularly and heavily on mandatory student fees to balance its budget does not meet the test of being successfully self-supporting. Not all athletics directors ascribe to this definition, however. A 1986 survey by the American Association of State Colleges and Universities (AASCU) asked member institutions "whether athletic programs generated revenue, were self-supporting, or operated at a deficit." Responses were mixed because they frequently included the comment that a program could be "self-supporting . . . with the help of student fees, or indirect state support through general university funds, or indirect state funds" (AASCU 1986, pp. 1–2).

AASCU's survey is important because it shows the relative inability of even Division I intercollegiate programs to fund varsity sports from ticket sales, contributions from alumni, and television revenues. Only nine of 60 responding Division I institutions reported that their athletics programs generated [net] revenue. Ticket sales, contributions, and television/radio contracts represented 30.5 percent of program funding (AASCU 1986, pp. 2–4). The questions then become, Who subsidizes the shortfalls on these activities? Are these subsidies congruent with sound educational and institutional policies? (Blackburn and Nyikos 1974; Lucey 1982; Nelson 1982, p. 49). And do the real and symbolic benefits of subsidized programs warrant the subsidies? If a university wishes to subsidize an expensive, money-losing Division I varsity sports program because its winning teams bring favorable publicity, symbolic stature, and the ubiquitous intangible benefits to the institution, then it should be clearly acknowledged by halting the misleading practice of calling varsity sports a self-supporting auxiliary enterprise. Instead, it would be more accurate to define the athletics department as a public service, an extension program devoted to cultivating good will—but possibly housed under university relations (Barnes, Rice, and Sturrock 1981, p. 12).

But what about those important, exceptional cases where Division I intercollegiate sports programs show a substantial surplus each year? An interesting example in 1988 was the University of Kentucky Athletic Association, which donated $4 million to the educational budget for the entire university. At first glance, this largesse appears to be a laudable effort. But it is disconcerting, because the UKAA tail could be wagging the university dog. Especially in a year when the state legislature granted faculty raises of only 2.5 percent and minimal funding for library and capital improvements, UKAA's affluence suggests practices and policies that do not fulfill the spirit of regional accreditation standards. The imbalance stands out even more when one considers that UKAA recently completed construction of a $6 million indoor football practice facility. A more substantive proposal for reform is that such one-time generosity of an athletics foundation perhaps could be modified to create a permanent relationship with the host institution. The athletics program at the University of Oklahoma, for example, pays 2 percent overhead to the university (Goodwin 1986, p. 84). Herein lies the genesis of one policy reform.

One option at Division I institutions is that the intercollegiate athletics program be treated comparably to sponsored research and development grants. Because it is the charter, the name, the logo, and the facilities of the university that make the special sports activity possible, the university could impose an internal tax on all revenues and donations brought in by varsity sports, which is not unlike the overhead that universities charge the federal government (often about 60 percent) on sponsored research grants. This mechanism would formally and systematically ensure that athletics programs carry through on one of their own traditional claims: that fund raising for athletics and a major varsity sports program systematically benefit the entire institution.

Changes in policies and practices, however, hinge upon a critical dimension of institutional self-study and redefinition. Universities with big-time sports programs should be required to recognize intercollegiate athletics as a substantial activity central to the university's mission and purpose (Hanford 1976, pp. 234–35), and it should be clearly stated in the charter and the mission statements a campus prepares for regional accreditation and for filing with such bodies as the state council on higher education (Fischer 1975, pp. 43–51).

FROM EDUCATION TO ENTERTAINMENT:
Public Policy and Intercollegiate Athletics Programs

The Arena of Government Oversight

The preceding section analyzed the hypothesis that moral outrage about the incipient big-business character of college
sports was neither sufficient nor especially effective as a strategy for analysis or reform and noted that even many major
athletics programs are pursuing financial practices that are
risky and often outright bad business. The next concern is
the related yet distinct question of whether financial practices
used by colleges and universities to support varsity sports are
sound public policy.

This section continues discussion of the economics and
finances of big-time college sports with a distinctive perspective: attention to points where an institution's intercollegiate
athletics program intersects with such external bodies as
municipal governments, state and federal agencies, legislatures, and the courts. They are the "cross pressures" (Miller
1982, p. 92) where athletics departments are free to behave
as they wish, but where at the same time external agencies
may in turn modify how they view colleges. Colleges and universities historically have enjoyed status as privileged institutions. State and federal governments provide exemptions,
and for the most part relations have been cordial. A few items
noted in the preceding section on the finances and economics
of intercollegiate athletics, however, carry beyond the realm
of institutional practices into the broader sphere of policy and
law (Grant 1979). In other words, current practices in big-
time college sports programs may lead to scrutiny on the basis
of state and federal policies (Fischer 1975, pp. 1–4; Lowell
1979; SHEEO 1988).

Intercollegiate athletics illustrates well shifting governmen-
tal attitudes toward colleges and universities. Corporations
and colleges have essentially changed seats since about 1900
in their respective positions with the federal government
(Glazer 1979). While antitrust legislation at the turn of the
century sought to control and prescribe business practices,
public policy sought to protect and exempt colleges and universities from external restraints and obligations. By 1980, this
situation had changed: Federal policy seeks increasingly to
stimulate corporate enterprise by deregulation, while at the
same time colleges and universities are increasingly expected
to comply with federal regulations and to be accountable for
internal practices (El-Khawas 1979; Grant 1979). The obvious

The case for invoking academic freedom becomes less compelling as academic institutions increasingly choose to behave like businesses.

area where this change comes to mind is in such personnel matters as affirmative action, environmental safety, and social security taxes. The burdens of accountability and compliance have indeed led to concern and rebuttal by the universities. Universities are justifiably concerned that federal policies from numerous, disparate agencies do not jeopardize the classic freedoms of what shall be taught, who shall be taught, and who shall teach (Bok 1980).

The case for invoking academic freedom becomes less compelling as academic institutions increasingly choose to behave like businesses. Twenty-five years ago, the "multiversity" and the "knowledge industry" were introduced (Kerr 1963). And it is no exaggeration when a community speaks of the local campus as its "largest smokeless industry." Johns Hopkins University, for example, is the largest employer in the city of Baltimore, Brown University makes the same claim for Providence, and Harvard ranks behind the government as the largest institutional employer in the Boston area. Little wonder, then, that such size, complexity, and diversification lead government agencies increasingly to treat the campus as an industry or business. It is the organizational evolution that has led to gradual yet persistent reduction of the traditional exemption from taxation and regulation that colleges and universities have enjoyed in the United States. Whether or not the claim that big-time college sports has become big business alters the place of sports *within* the institution is for each campus to decide (Fischer 1975, pp. 1–2; Hanford 1976, pp. 232–35). Universities may be assured, however, that such self-descriptions are consequential in how the courts, the Internal Revenue Service, the U.S. Congress, and state legislatures and city councils henceforth view the American campus.

The Relationship between Town and Gown: The Local Economy and the Public Policy of Property Taxation

One frequent justification of college spectator sports is the area of town/gown relations (Alberger 1981). A winning team with a large stadium is said to be a source of state and civic pride; often cited is the fact that when the home team plays, the population swells—such that Memorial Stadium in Lincoln, Nebraska, on game day becomes "the third largest city in the state" or Corvallis becomes the fifth largest city in Oregon on football game days for Oregon State University (Michener 1976). Games are popular and good for the local economy, measured in terms of revenues from food, beverages, hotel rooms, and so on. A small but growing body of data challenges the hegemony of this rationale, however: Big-time entertainment puts a strain on city services. Problems of parking, police, security, supervision, and strained city budgets signal that when colleges venture into large-scale spectator events, they may jeopardize some of the local tax exemption and privileges that historically they have taken for granted.

Success brings scrutiny. Colleges will be hard pressed in the future to maintain their present level of revenues from varsity sports for another reason: the prospect of limitations on spectator events. As city governments face deficits, they may consider whether university-sponsored spectator events held in a campus facility are in fact "educational activities" worthy of tax exemption. It could include city taxes on stadia and arenas, as has happened at the Carrier Dome in Syracuse (Kirby 1988) and at Cornell University (Blumenstyk 1988). Thus far, such municipal taxation has tended to be confined to commercial events, but when college sports become commercialized, they may also be subject to the same kinds of restraints and responsibilities as, for instance, rock concerts.

To put the issue to the litmus test, consider whether an intercollegiate football game or basketball game truly constitutes an "educational activity" (Blackburn and Nyikos 1974; Fischer 1975, pp. 1–4). Or whether revenues from the activity go to support primarily bona fide academic or educational activities. As college sports become increasingly professionalized and are financially and structurally distinct from the academic administration and curriculum, colleges may be hard pressed to fulfill either criterion (Frey 1982, pp. 224–26). Colleges are caught in a bind in that increasingly they lease such campus facilities for expressly noncollege functions to bring in revenues, all of which tends further to weaken the argument that they are "educational facilities." Why should a college-owned facility used for commercial events be worthy of exemption from property taxes when a comparable facility owned by a corporation is not? (Blumenstyk 1988; Kirby 1988).

Tax Laws: Athletics Foundations and Unrelated Business Purposes

While exemption from property taxes is the crucial issue in relations with local governments, colleges and universities face another area of eroding privileges when dealing with the federal government. Government officials who interpret federal law look at the *nature* of activities pursued by nonprofit educational organizations that claim tax-exempt status under section 501(c)(3) of the Internal Revenue Code (Wong 1988, p. 637). Hence, when a campus student center includes a travel agency or a store that sells computers and clothing, the test is how these activities differ from a commercial enterprise. In short, why should a college enterprise automatically be tax exempt as a 501 organization when its parts are admittedly commercial? Furthermore, the inquiry is kindled by travel agencies and stationery and clothing stores that predictably and justifiably see exemption for the university as an unfair advantage (Jaschik 1988). This general scrutiny of unrelated business income tax is especially pertinent to the relationship of intercollegiate athletics programs to the overall mission (and tax exemption) of the institution (Thelin 1978, p. 182).

Thus, we return to an obvious but important feature described in the preceding section: Many colleges and universities have opted to operate intercollegiate athletics programs as separately chartered and incorporated athletics/educational foundations (Barnes 1981; Callahan 1981; Miller 1981), suggesting a legal entity that, although related to the structure of the university, is distinct and has varying degrees of autonomous operation and purpose. Moving college sports into an incorporated "foundation" obviously has some gains for fund raising and for independence from university oversight. But it leaves the corporation open to the question of what it has to do with tax-exempt educational activities. To the extent that intercollegiate sports becomes an increasingly self-contained enterprise whose fund raising goes for the explicit end of funding athletic teams and contests, athletics officials will be hard pressed to justify their corporation as being related to the university's academic and educational goals (Frey 1982, pp. 224–28).

One significant determinant is found in the public statements by athletics directors and coaches that they see their intercollegiate teams as "entertainment" and as "big business." Such claims may give them license to operate in some ways, but at the same time they cause college sports to drift from the protective moorings of an educational, nonprofit tax-exempt organization. The IRS exempts educational activities but not professional entertainment. Colleges and universities, then, are susceptible to increased taxation for their "unrelated business purposes" (Wong 1988, pp. 637–47) and their "commingled purposes" (Weistart 1983–84). As universities choose to combine educational and entertainment activities, the clarity of nonprofit tax exemption for them becomes muddied.

To better assess whether an athletics department activity is subject to unrelated business income taxation, it is important for the high school and college athletics administrator to understand the general principles and issues in determining whether the activity constitutes a trade or business regularly carried on and not substantially related to the exercise and performance of the institution's educational function. An activity will be classified as a trade or business if it is "carried on for the production of income from the sale of goods or the performance of services." The activity does not lose identity as a trade or business merely because it is carried on within the larger aggregate of similar activities. In other words, a business activity is not made otherwise by association with charitable (e.g., educational) operations. Additionally, the absence of profits does not necessarily eliminate the possibility of taxation. Instead, it is the quest for profit *that is decisive* (Wong 1988, p. 641).

Colleges, of course, counter that athletics/educational foundations are integral to the institution's *educational* mission. But this argument will be disputed on two grounds: *governance* and *exclusivity* (Blackburn and Nyikos 1974, pp. 110–11). Most athletics foundations have their own board of directors, apart from the college or university's board, which strengthens the IRS's case that athletics foundations are separate creatures in form and content from the college (Lederman 1988c, p. A41). Second, varsity athletics facilities at institutions with big-time sports programs are for the most part for exclusive use by the varsity athletes, coaches, athletics department staff, and donors (Blackburn and Nyikos 1974; Sack 1982, pp. 82–83). To test the prognosis, consider whether a typical student or faculty member can gain access to playing fields, courts, or lockers in the varsity sports complex. Construction of special dormitories for athletes stands as another practice that increases the distance between athletes and students when a nonprofit organization is reviewed for tax pur-

poses. Athletics departments offer substantial tutoring and academic support services—no doubt an "educational" service—but even this service is suspect if it is reserved for use by and for that small group of students that also are varsity athletes receiving grants-in-aid based on athletic ability (Fischer 1975). Such varieties of exclusivity cast doubt on athletics foundations' claims that they serve students or are part of student life. In fact, their facilities exist to enhance and perpetuate the distinct activities of intercollegiate sports. And the appearance of "exclusivity" would be more pronounced as intercollegiate athletics departments drop "nonrevenue" sports in favor of maintaining a handful of "major" sports. Offering fewer varsity sports means that a smaller, more homogeneous group of students is accommodated as varsity athletes. The athletics director who balances the budget by dropping women's field hockey, for example, will be hard pressed to claim the sports program serves all student athletic interests. Furthermore, expenses for *recruiting* future athletes are not part of the tax-exempt framework for charitable or educational organizations: "Raising funds to be used for travel and other activities to interview and persuade prospective students with outstanding athletic ability to attend a particular university does not evidence an exempt purpose" (Wong 1988, p. 639).

Not only will a university risk its tax-exempt status if it operates its foundation for entertainment; it will also be increasingly susceptible at another point: Incentives of tax exemption for donors are diminishing. The traditional adage for fund raising for college sports has been, "To raise money from prospective donors, you have to spend money on prospective donors." Or, as one athletics fund raiser reported, "In athletic fund raising, you're really selling a product . . . something that a person can feel and grasp" (Bennett 1981, p. 1). A good example of how this principle has been put into practice comes from Clemson University:

> *Clemson's first condominium parking garage opens this fall for football fans willing to spend $10,000 to $12,000 to tailgate in style. For the money, a fan gets car space and access to a large-screen television, dance floor, and wet bar. . . . The project, to be constructed in a remodeled laundry building, will have 95 parking spaces and a 4,000–square foot pavilion a quarter-mile from the stadium (The Washington Post 27 August 1987).*

Many fund-raising brochures for university athletics foundations note that donations are "fully tax deductible" because they are charitable contributions for educational purposes. Not so. Federal tax reform increasingly emphasizes that a taxpayer cannot claim a deduction for portions of a charitable contribution for which one receives demonstrable benefits (Bernstein 1986, pp. 93–94). Hence, for the parking space at Clemson, one would have to subtract the fair market value of the tickets, the parking privileges, the special seating, the entertainment, and the food. The net effect is that such tax reform will make college sports less attractive to donors as a charitable tax deduction (Sage 1982).

The case of Clemson may be extreme, but it is hardly exceptional. Virtually every college athletics foundation has gradations of perks calibrated to the amount of one's annual gift. The face value of a ticket often is not what a sports fan pays for a scarce seat at a college game. One must make a donation or join a club for the opportunity to purchase a ticket (Barnes, Rice, and Sturrock 1981, pp. 12–13). A good sample comes from the University of Kentucky's Blue and White Fund in 1987: starting with a basic donation of $40 per year and rising to $10,000 and up, the benefits for donations start with a Blue and White membership card and increase correspondingly with auto decals, *Cat Tales* magazine, a poster, recognition in the program, priority seating for football and basketball games, press guides, free parking for football games, first opportunity to purchase two tickets to selected games, first opportunity to purchase tickets to tournaments, bowls, and away games, VIP parking for football games, pregame parties (by invitation only), an invitation to the Blue Room and the Wildcat Den, a University of Kentucky blue blazer, a party invitation from the athletics director, and special travel privileges with teams.

This example is typical of Division I fund-raising strategies (Alberger 1981, pp. 84–97). And the IRS is not the only government agency that shows increasing concern about athletics/educational foundations (Frey 1982, pp. 224–26; Sage 1982, p. 141). State governments too have started to ask more searching questions about foundations' operations and financial, legal, and personnel practices, with the Washington state council on higher education representing exemplary statewide policy analysis (Fischer 1975). The case of Virginia provides a model of responsible and concerned state government review. In 1982, the commonwealth's attorney general, Gerald L. Baliles, wrote to the president of each public college to express concern about legal problems posed by the policies of fund raising associated with state-supported colleges and universities. He suggested, "In an era of diminishing financial resources, the General Assembly may wish to take a closer look at financial practices of such foundations" (see also *Hampton Roads Daily Press* 3 June 1982). According to the attorney general, "There is little knowledge or understanding of those foundations and, in some instances, little if any accountability" for millions of dollars they raise and spend. After alluding to "several legal problems" related to the foundations, he asked presidents to consider several questions:

- Who manages "investments and application of funds" on behalf of the foundation?
- Do members of institutions' boards of visitors also serve on foundations' boards?
- Do the institutions receive regular reports from foundations on the foundation's receipts and expenditures and financial condition?
- What authority does the institution have over removal of directors or officers of the foundation?
- Are any or all of the employees of the foundation either considered state employees or receiving such state benefits as insurance and supplemental retirement benefits?
- What means do institutions use to monitor funds held by a foundation in trust for the institution?
- Are funds for "educational foundations" included in the universitywide budgeting process for intercollegiate athletics?

Such review does not mean that athletics foundations are necessarily doing anything wrong. But it shows that foundations to this point have been somewhat unknown and uncontrolled entities with few mechanisms to ensure adequate reporting and fidelity to the institution's purposes (Frey 1982, pp. 224–30). The issue does not go away; in 1988, for example, several states, among them Wisconsin, Oklahoma, Connecticut, and Oregon, initiated inquiries comparable to those in Virginia as "reports of misuse prompt[ed] widespread investigations of public colleges' private fund-raising arms (Blumenstyk 1989; McMillen 1988).

From Accountability to Compliance:
Paying the Price of Nonprofit Status

The protections and exemptions a college gains from its status
as a nonprofit educational organization increasingly carry obligations. And obligations—especially in the form of compliance with state and federal regulations—will most likely
increase the costs associated with operating intercollegiate
sports programs (Lowell 1979; Miller 1982, pp. 101–2). Obvious areas of increasing costs are liability insurance for athletic
injuries, equitable funding and facilities for the sexes in compliance with Title IX, litigation involving violations of student
rights, compliance with health and safety regulations in the
construction and renovation of athletic facilities, increased
record keeping on such matters as athletes' graduation rates,
and provision of drug-testing programs. Furthermore, incidents of scandal involving slush funds for booster clubs probably indicate increased bonding requirements and liability
for board members of athletics foundations. These cumulative
added costs, most of which were either small or nonexistent
10 to 15 years ago, are sufficient to erode the surplus revenues
seemingly prosperous programs make (Frey 1982, p. 231;
Koch 1971).

Direct State Monies:
Public Policy and Intercollegiate Athletics

Issues of tax exemption and compliance with regulations represent real yet indirect "costs" and "subsidies" for college athletics programs. Although some major athletics programs are
truly self-supporting, a significant number of states provide
some form of funding and resources for varsity sports programs. Florida, for example, provides direct and indirect
appropriations for women's varsity sports (Palmer 1981).
Washington provides for the administration of varsity sports
programs as part of student services for those varsity teams
that do not rely on subsidized recruitment and athletic grants-
in-aid (Fischer 1975). AASCU's survey of athletics programs
indicates that among 60 responding Division I member institutions, 20 receive direct state support for intercollegiate
sports, constituting 38 percent of athletics program budgets
at those 20 institutions (AASCU 1986, pp. 2–3). These exceptions to the rule of self-support have become increasingly controversial and volatile in the past few years.

Oregon provides the most interesting case for understanding how the expenses of intercollegiate athletics can be transformed from a matter of institutional practice to one of public policy. Shortfalls in revenues for the three major public universities (Oregon, Oregon State, and Portland State) have led to the proposed elimination of some sports, following the example of Washington State University, which eliminated its varsity swimming team as an economy measure in 1975 (Fischer 1975, p. 8). State law in Oregon (like in Washington and Florida) prohibits direct subsidies to intercollegiate athletics (Barnes 1981; Fischer 1975). The circular logic is that college sports can be good for the state's economy but only if the state directs substantial tax monies to varsity sports programs at the state universities (Palmer 1981, p. 73). Legislators are caught in a bind: that such an option coexists with a weak state economy and competing demands for secondary schools, health care, and social services, to name a few (Lederman 1988d). The state of Oregon resolved this tension with a compromise: Neither tax monies nor mandatory student fees would go for intercollegiate athletics; however, starting in September 1989, proceeds from a state-sponsored National Football League lottery will generate money for varsity sports programs at the state's public colleges and universities (Associated Press 1989b). In terms of public policy in most states, however, a central, enduring concern is that while the state legislature and council work to keep both taxes and tuition low, an institution might offset it by imposing self-determined fees on students (Frey 1982, pp. 230–32).

Independent colleges and universities of course have great freedom in budget determinations and allocations. Whether the board of trustees of a private university decides that tuition charges ought to cover special programs, whether international studies or intercollegiate athletics, is no matter of public policy. State law and public institutions are another matter, as many states explicitly prohibit that tuition and tax monies go for auxiliary enterprises. Yet even in those states that prohibit tax monies' going to public colleges for support of varsity sports, another tactic of sorts allows for sports subsidies. In many states, public colleges and universities are permitted to levy a mandatory student activities fee. Although it is legally separate from the charge for tuition, often it is levied and published as a single amount that combines both tuition and fee (AASCU 1986; SHEEO 1988).

For those public institutions whose athletics programs have

little prospect of substantial revenues from television or contributions from major donors, the student activity fee has become an increasingly attractive option for balancing the varsity sports budget (Fullerton 1985, pp. 16–18; Palmer 1981, pp. 70–71). It is an option that raises questions of institutional policy—and, for state universities, public policy. What are the proper criteria for using student fees to subsidize varsity athletics programs?

Many institutions do so—but at a fairly small rate per capita. At the University of Colorado, for example, the student fee per semester for 1987–88 was $19.75 per student toward intercollegiate athletics. Although the practice has caused some controversy among students at Colorado, its scope pales in comparison to smaller public universities with comprehensive varsity programs. In Division I-A schools with medium-size student bodies (from about 5,000 to 15,000), the temptation to rely on the student activity fee to support intercollegiate athletics is great (AASCU 1986, pp. 2–3; SHEEO 1988).

At one public institution, however, mandatory student fees for 1988–89 of about $700 per year included $518 earmarked for intercollegiate athletics, and student fees represented over 60 percent of the athletics department's budget, even though the department has a fund-raising foundation, a 15,000-seat football stadium, and an 11,000-seat basketball arena. This practice raises the question of whether college sports should take such a large percentage of student fees, which of course cuts down on money for other activities. Furthermore, one returns to a familiar sticking point: Varsity sports and their facilities are not open to all students (Lipper 1987; Newsom 1988).

The student fee becomes a matter of public policy when it is a substantial percentage of mandatory charges. An official college catalog merely lists a single charge, "tuition and general fee," of $2,700. The lump sum masks the inordinate subsidy that goes to college sports—at the expense of students and their parents. In itself it is a dubious practice that skirts the spirit of responsible consumerism. In this case, tuition of $2,000 per academic year plus the $700 mandatory fee total $2,700 for an in-state undergraduate. Thus, intercollegiate athletics represents almost 20 percent of the official charges to each in-state student, a practice that raises questions with legislators and with the state council of higher education. Such institutional self-determination increases the price of higher

The student fee becomes a matter of public policy when it is a substantial percentage of mandatory charges.

education, perhaps undoing the work of the legislature to keep educational charges down. Left untended, such practices ultimately represent questionable educational policy (AASCU 1986; SHEEO 1988).

This interpretation is not mere conjecture. The following observation suggests how funding for intercollegiate athletics is working to the fore of state policy issues, with added implications for states' student financial aid programs:

> *Colleges and universities compete for student enrollments and for public support by offering a wide variety of services and facilities that are at best indirectly related to higher education: intercollegiate athletics, with stadiums and coliseums; health services; entertainment; and so on. These services and facilities are supported by mandatory fees. In some Virginia institutions, such fees have increased far more rapidly than the cost of living over the last 10 years.*
>
> *Students and their parents, as consumers, appear to want many if not all of these services and facilities. But they may not realize the price they pay for them. In addition, both state and federal governments pay for them through financial aid programs based on need. Finally, mandatory fees for peripheral services may extract a large hidden social cost if they prohibit young women and men from attending college. . . .*
>
> *Student financial aid should not be used to pay for peripheral activities and services for which fees are charged. At present, for instance, support for intercollegiate athletics is built into a general fee, which in turn is considered in determining how much financial aid a student needs. Both state and federal financial aid are being used to support services and activities unrelated to the major missions of higher education* (Davies 1987, pp. 19–20).

Colleges and the Courts: The Case of Television
Most institutions tend to see their annual budgeting problems as set by their own particular situation. This view can be myopic because developments in public policy occasionally swiftly and dramatically alter the environment in which *all* institutions operate. Nowhere is this situation better illustrated than in litigation involving television contracts for intercollegiate athletics.

One such event happened in 1984 when the universities of Oklahoma and Georgia successfully sued the NCAA to gain the right of self-determination in televising games. As the chair of the NCAA's football television committee noted in a special report:

For the first football season since NBC purchased television rights from the National Collegiate Athletic Association for $1,144,000 in 1952, the NCAA Football Television Committee was not responsible for administering a national plan in 1984.

The United States Supreme Court voided on June 27 the Association's contracts with ABC Sports, CBS Sports, and the Entertainment and Sports Programming Network (ESPN), which would have been worth nearly $74 million. The Television Committee prepared a new television plan for the consideration of the Division I-A and I-AA membership, and this option was defeated 44–66–1 in a roll call vote of the Division I-A membership at a special meeting in Chicago on July 10 (NCAA 1985, p. 3).

This action dissolved the NCAA/ABC monopoly on televising NCAA member games, with two major consequences. Under the old rules, the NCAA carefully restricted the number of times a given team could appear on a national or regional broadcast; second, revenues were shared and television schedules distributed with concern for diffusing and sharing the wealth. At the same time, the effect of such policies was to restrain those university teams that had the potential to command strong viewing audiences. The 1984 suit opened the floodgates for university teams and networks to negotiate their own television arrangements, which worked to the benefit of, for example, the University of Oklahoma, the University of Georgia, the Atlantic Coast Conference, the Southeastern Conference, the Southwestern Conference, and most members of the elite Central Football Association—at least over the short run (Frey 1982, pp. 229–30; Oberlander 1988a).

Four years after the landmark legal triumph, even highly successful and affluent programs observed that television had ceased to be an assured lucrative outlet. In June 1988, for example, the athletics director at UCLA pointed to 1983 as the high point for UCLA's television revenues (Bonk 1988). So although the argument is quite correct that the Court's decision in 1984 ended the (unfair) cartel of NCAA policy (Lawrence 1987b, pp. 104–8), the victory for individual institutional self-determination is not a clear financial triumph. The ensuing saturation of television markets with college football games means that television stations and networks know that most college games will have decreasing appeal to viewers. Less than five years after the successful suit, Central Football Association members themselves have discussed self-imposed restrictions on television schedules.

Concerns over plummeting television ratings and fees have prompted a series of meetings between a group of athletics directors from colleges that play big-time football and representatives of athletic conferences, television networks, and sports associations. The meetings could lead to the formation of an umbrella group that would [negotiate TV contracts] . . . for most colleges. Such a move could bring some order to what many athletics officials have called a "chaotic" marketplace for televised football that has existed since 1984, when the Supreme Court ruled that the National Collegiate Athletic Association's contract as exclusive bargaining agent for its members violated federal antitrust laws (Oberlander 1988a, p. A37).

The puzzle of college sports finances is also shown by a second major television windfall. Big-time college basketball programs acquired unexpected large resources about 15 years ago when the "Final Four" and preceding elimination games in the NCAA's postseason tournament came to be televised to national and regional audiences. In 1978, the television contract for the NCAA basketball tournament consisted of 32 teams playing over 18 dates with television revenues of about $5 million. Those numbers have increased dramatically so that in 1986 the tournament included 64 teams, 34 dates, and about $33 million in television revenue. Revenues in 1988 were $57.8 million, but the NCAA estimates television revenues in 1989 to decline to $55.4 million—a figure that supports a projection made by the commissioner of the Big East Conference in 1988: "I don't see TV rights escalating as they have in the past two negotiations because the programming format is already maximized" (Associated Press 1988a; Taaffe 1986).

Important for planning is the indication that the television sports market has probably peaked—and even big-time teams are unlikely to receive a bonanza. The strategy then becomes for a Division I team to attempt to make the Final Four in basketball or to receive a bid to a major, televised bowl game in football. Even though individual institutions may beat the odds, college football and basketball teams as a whole are probably confined to a no-growth arena characterized by an increasingly imbalanced distribution of profits.

The television environment is precarious (Frey 1982, pp. 229-35). Looking beyond college sports to the broader sphere of *all* televised sports, the major networks face severe financial problems. In 1985, two of the three networks lost a combined $35 million to $50 million in sports programming, with only CBS showing a profit. Network executives contend they can no longer pay high fees for broadcast rights. And the glut of sports programming means an increasing number of "traditional" TV events will no longer be broadcast (Taafe 1986). The Rose Bowl, the NCAA basketball final four, and other premier events are probably not among the endangered species, but some fallout is already apparent for second-tier national events, including the Gator Bowl and the Blue Bonnet Bowl, which are having difficulty finding sponsors. The traditional Fiesta Bowl in El Paso in 1990 will become the John Hancock Bowl to showcase the insurance company's sponsorship. Weakening the college football bowls puts in motion a domino effect. Without national television coverage plus corporate sponsorship, postseason bowl games are unable to offer college teams large sums for playing, dismantling the colleges' strategy in bowl games as a sure way to raise revenues (Sage 1982, p. 141).

The Netherworld Economy of College and School Sports

State legislatures, attorneys general, and the IRS have reason to be concerned about a college sports economy that is both large and often unaccountable (Gerber 1979). One concern is that most budgets for intercollegiate athletics tend to be low estimates of actual monies involved (Atwell, Grimes, and Lopiano 1980, pp. 30-37). Annual departmental budgets are operating budgets and as such tend to understate the resources and space that universities provide varsity sports. Recurrent scandals turn up evidence of slush funds from booster clubs, large amounts of monies that are unreported and illegal. Fur-

ther, institutional analyses of college athletics are limited in that they tend to overlook the vast netherworld of the economy of amateur sports; while indicating affluence they also illustrate resources that seldom accrue to host colleges and universities. The cumulative product of these disparate, often unofficial or unreported enterprises constitutes a netherworld of intercollegiate sports that matches closely what has been identified as "the underground economy" of college athletics (Hart-Nibbrig and Cottingham 1986, pp. 63–68). Among those enterprises are summer all-star games for high school and college players, recruiting and rating services, agents and representatives for college athletes, product endorsements, coaches' summer camps, gambling (and related information services), souvenirs, and capital improvements.

It matters little that the college basketball season is seven months long, starts in October, and ends with the Final Four in April. Scholastic and college basketball fans can enjoy such events as the McDonald's High School All-Star game in mid-April, broadcast by ABC "live from 'The Pit' at the University of New Mexico" and promoted by full-page advertisements in *Sports Illustrated* and spots on network television. Graduating high school seniors headed for major college teams get to see and be seen at numerous events—the Nike/ABCD All-American Camp held each summer at Princeton University or the annual Dapper Dan High School All-Star game in Pittsburgh, for example (Brubaker 1988).

The grease for this postseason athletic machinery comes from manufacturers, often athletic shoe companies. According to a report in *The Washington Post,* "The most influential man in the world of high school basketball may be a paunchy, 48-year-old former player-agent and one-time Las Vegas gambler who works for the Nike shoe and apparel company" (Brubaker 1988). When a reporter says this shoe company representative has clout, he means that 80 major college basketball coaches are under contract with Nike to endorse Nike basketball shoes, with the agreement that their varsity players will wear Nikes. Endorsement contracts can be as low as $5,000, but they usually are substantially higher. One college basketball coach is reported to receive $100,000 per year from a shoe company.

This situation leads to "the college coach as entrepreneur" (Sperber 1987). The "model" coach commands an official salary higher than eminent professors and, in a number of cases, higher than the university president. The salary is accompanied by substantial perks and commercial endorsements. The varsity basketball coach at North Carolina State, for example, has an estimated annual income over $500,000, drawn from a base annual salary of $85,000 (attached to a 10-year contract that runs until 1993), "about $100,000 a year and other perks from Nike shoes," a fee for each of 40 to 50 speeches per year of $5,000 an appearance, endorsements of various commercial products, three television and radio shows, summer basketball camps, and royalties from books and video tapes. The university athletics department also gives him free football and basketball tickets, which he is free to sell for personal profit. The coach is "a busy man and to help him move about, he has the free use of three new cars."

Coaches negotiate interesting arrangements with their universities and athletics departments. Summer camps for various sports have become popular—and lucrative. The most troubling point for public policy is whether coaches pay fair rental fees for sponsoring sports camps at university facilities. At the University of Arizona, for example, the football coach pays $50 rent for the use of the football stadium, practice fields, and weight room. At the University of Maryland, former basketball coach Lefty Driesell's contract allowed him to continue to sponsor summer basketball camps on campus, which grossed $231,000 in 1986. The men's basketball coach at the University of Michigan is reported to have grossed over $350,000 for his 1986 summer camps (Sperber 1987).

Income is increased with supplementary benefits from the athletics foundation or from local boosters. Highly visible coaches receive numerous perks from their athletics departments or athletics/educational foundations—low-interest mortgages, cars, dues for country clubs and other organizations. An interesting footnote is that "universities, often public ones, resisted reporters' and researchers' attempts to obtain accurate figures on salaries and perquisites" (Sperber 1987, p. 33). The practices are not necessarily wrong or illegal; however, the first point of concern for state officials is simply having reliable information reported on such activities (Palmer 1981, pp. 65–66). A second point worth reemphasizing is that local car dealers who donate a car to the university coach or athletics foundation official often claim a tax deduction on the grounds that they donated it to a nonprofit educational institution (Bennett 1981, p. 9).

Governors' Interest in
Intercollegiate Athletics

From time to time, governors also assume the role as visible, real, and symbolic leaders who ought take responsibility for fostering the proper balance of academics and athletics in higher education most often assumed by college and university presidents. Certainly it is the case for flagship state universities, often described as "vital state resources" and a "tribute to the people of the state." Varsity championships by state university teams are in turn hailed as a "victory for the entire state" and a source of regional pride (Bennett 1981; Michener 1976, pp. 219–80).

The tone of gubernatorial leadership in higher education varies greatly of course in time and place. In the 1930s, Governor Huey Long's affiliation with Louisiana State University set a standard that has been difficult to surpass. College sports was at the heart of the attachment: Governor Long wrote the Tiger Rag varsity fight song, attended all LSU football games, regularly posed for photographs with coaches, teams, and cheerleaders, and even led the LSU band at half-time performances. To ensure fans' support for LSU's road games, he coerced railroads into offering low fares so that thousands of LSU students could travel to games throughout the region. Today that model persists, albeit in diluted form. More recently the governor of New Mexico joined with University of New Mexico administrators and board members in an unsuccessful attempt to recruit Indiana University's basketball coach, the rationale being that building a championship Division I basketball team constituted an invaluable rallying point for state morale.

Intercollegiate athletics is not always a rallying point for state unity, however. Often it may be a wedge that divides state constituencies, like rivalries between, say, Indiana and Purdue, the University of Kentucky and the University of Louisville, or the University of California at Berkeley and UCLA. Rivalries lead to competition for scarce resources, and often intrastate universities avoid playing one another. Nor is a governor's fondness for state university sports always limitless. Intercollegiate athletics has a divisive effect in the life of a state on another front: The publicity about excesses and scandals drains energy and resources from educational pursuits (Frey 1982, pp. 230–31). All too often state legislatures and elected officials are erroneously depicted as uncritical boosters, easily sway by such perks as tailgate parties, half-time salutes, and choice seats at big games. In fact, their ultimate concern is educational propriety, even educational excellence (Fischer 1975, pp. 1–4). Increasing scrutiny of intercollegiate athletics by state legislatures is suggested by the NCAA's report that as of May 1989, 183 bills "that might affect college sports programs or athletes [were] pending in state legislatures" (Lederman 1989). Recent incidents in Virginia illustrate the increased nationwide concern that provides a counter to the convenient stereotype of uncritical state boosterism.

On June 13, 1988, then-Governor Gerald Baliles delivered the commencement address at Virginia Polytechnic Institute and State University. For over a decade, the school had enjoyed laudable growth as a comprehensive flagship university, with impressive gains in research and development, diversification into arts and sciences, and the traditional institutional commitment to its land-grant charter. At the same time, educational expansion and improvement were accompanied by strong varsity athletics teams in football and basketball and in nonrevenue sports. Somewhere the balance between academics and athletics was lost, however. And the imbalance did not go unnoticed.

The governor declared in his speech, "Let no one doubt where I stand." And "by the time [he] finished his remarkably tough, blunt speech, there could be no doubt. His message was simple: Academics comes before athletics" (Newport News–Hampton (Virginia) *Daily Press,* 16 June 1987). Baliles told the commencement crowd, "We have glimpsed an ominous future, a future few of us ever thought possible. . . . It is a future of misspent financial resources, of million-dollar coaching contracts, and lavish expense accounts. It is a future that invites unethical conduct and humiliating publicity. . . . It is a future that Virginia Tech does not need" (Baliles 1987). He reminded university board members of their special and ultimate responsibility for institutional priorities. Instead of the ritualized good feelings customarily found between governors and their state university athletics teams, scandals and abuses had led to the governor's serious concern:

Something has happened here—something that could jeopardize this institution's long-held mission. . . . To the historic ambitions of educational excellence and research leadership held by this university, a new set of ambitions [has] been

*added—objectives that if allowed to grow unchecked could
easily compromise Virginia Tech's excellence and injure
its dreams.*

*These ambitions are not measured by breakthroughs in
research, but by breaking records in gate receipts. These are
ambitions not measured by the achievements of scholars,
but by glory on the playing field. While I do not condemn
those who hold these ambitions, I will tell you that they are
not mine* (Baliles 1987).

Although excellence in academics and sports could go
hand in hand, they could also be in conflict. The speech
received great applause from VPI alumni and was hailed in
newspapers throughout the state and the nation. It helped
set Baliles among government leaders concerned about educational priorities. State policy toward higher education is not
merely a matter of providing funds: It also includes responsible stewardship. Baliles's concern is unusual, and no indication exists that other governors have followed suit. He is,
however, influential, having served as chair of the National
Governors Association in 1988. Such a national forum could
make this example intriguing to other states where intercollegiate athletics in the public universities has become imbalanced (Blumenstyk 1988, 1989).

Presidents and Intercollegiate Athletics

"Three things can happen, and two of them are bad," said legendary football coach Woody Hayes of the forward pass. University presidents have come to regard intercollegiate athletics with equal apprehension. College sports is risky business (Hanford 1976, pp. 232–35), and academic lore is full of unpleasant stories about university presidents who have been forced out by athletic imbroglios (Davis 1979, p. 420). As one president bluntly said, "I just want to keep athletics off the *front* page."

Most college and university presidents support a strong varsity sports program as an outlet for students, an attraction for alumni, and a public relations benefit for the institution (Lowell 1979, p. 482; Nelson 1982, p. 53; Rudolph 1962, pp. 373–93). A president probably can entertain and influence more people at the Big Game than at any other event except perhaps commencement (Barnes 1981, p. 58; Cady 1978, pp. 209–10). Even harsh critics of big-time athletics acknowledge the legitimacy of college sports. "Its place in the educational enterprise is not simply legitimate but essential" (Atwell 1985, p. 395). Presidents who do not vigorously endorse a strong program usually do not oppose it either (Nelson 1982, pp. 52–55)—at least not before the home crowd.

Presidents spend considerable time off campus talking with alumni and other supporters. Seldom do such conversations escape the query, "How's the team going to do this year?" The question is expected, even desired, because it opens possibilities for discussion. After a few comments about the team's expected improvement or its continued winning ways (depending on last year's record), the president invariably connects athletics with academics. In fact, many presidents use such conversations as evidence that visible athletics teams are good for universities because they attract attention and generate interest (Nelson 1982). And, of course, alumni especially want to hear and even believe the ubiquitous claim, "We win with real students" (Sack 1982).

Those who support intercollegiate athletics state, at least *publicly,* that academics and athletics need not detract from one another (Bennett 1981, p. 7). Most see no intrinsic incompatibility between excellence in athletics and excellence in academics and advance the theory that athletes earn their best grades during their sports season. Stanford, Duke, Michigan, Virginia, North Carolina, and Notre Dame are universities often

External presidents and external athletics are perhaps the most visible university symbols—and a winning symbol is preferable to a losing one.

cited as proof that big-time athletics and academics can mix successfully (Gilley and Hickey 1986, pp. 5–6).

Not everyone agrees with this litany (Silber, quoted in Nelson 1982, p. 56). Some passionate disbelievers claim presidents are touting an impossibility because the goals of U.S. higher education and big-time athletics are incompatible (Lawrence 1987b; Rooney 1987; Scott 1956, pp. 29–32). They believe athletics has become excessive, has distorted the university's mission, and has tarnished the integrity of all higher education (McGuff 1989). If it is so, presidents have work to do.

Presidents—the one figure everyone, supporters and critics alike, agrees upon—must assume ultimate responsibility for maintaining the proper balance between academics and athletics (American Council on Education 1979, pp. 347–49; Hanford 1976, pp. 232–35).

> *Presidents can control athletics if they have the will, the inclination, and the desire. The proper balance between athletics and academics cannot be achieved by the NCAA, but can be achieved by each president or chancellor on his or her campus, deciding what the campus should be, an academic institution or an entertainment capital* (Raymond M. Burse, quoted in Lederman 1987a, pp. 32–33).

Presidents, then, are in charge—or ought to be (American Council on Education 1979, pp. 347–49). The idea is not new. Sixty years ago, the president of the Carnegie Foundation for the Advancement of Teaching wrote about campus athletics programs, "There can be no doubt as to where lies the responsibility to correct this situation. Defense of the intellectual integrity of the colleges and universities lies with the president and faculty" (Pritchett, quoted in Savage et al. 1929, pp. xx–xxi). Presidents claim they can do the job (Gilley and Hickey 1986, pp. 3–5), and they think there is a job to be done. A recent survey of presidents of institutions in the NCAA's Division I showed that 70 percent "expressed confidence that university presidents can resolve the athletic dilemma by simply taking control" (Gilley and Hickey 1986, pp. 3–6).

Malaise over intercollegiate athletics has been present for over a century, with periodic acute attacks like those of the present (Hardy and Berryman 1982, pp. 15–28). If everyone agrees that presidents should "do something," and presidents believe they can, what is the holdup? (Kerr 1963, p. 16). Is it that nobody knows what to do, or that they cannot agree on what ought to be done? Is it that they are working on the problem, albeit slowly? Or is the dilemma that "doing something" about athletics carries great personal risk for a president who has many other important things to do? (Frey 1982).

For presidents, intercollegiate athletics often is a no-win proposition. No matter what happens, someone is visibly and vocally upset, thus leading to the syndrome of "presidential inattention" (Hanford 1976). After all, sports are part of the American character, often described as a "secular religion" and readily part of our nation's political metaphors (Balbus 1975). They are central to the liturgy of the American "booster college" (Bennett 1981, pp. 3–5; Boorstin 1965). Witness the promotion of the Olympics or the statewide frenzy when the home team makes the Super Bowl. On local television stations every night across the nation, news, weather, *and* sports constitute the day's events. *USA Today,* the nation's most widely read newspaper, has four sections, one of which is sports (Hart-Nibbrig and Cottingham 1986, pp. 33–54). Our country's obsession with sports makes Americans passionately interested in the contests and the athletes themselves. Colleges and universities share in this distinctively American appetite. And college presidents cannot escape being caught in the middle of such enthusiasm (Flexner 1930, pp. 65–66; Rudolph 1962, pp. 373–93; Veysey 1964, p. 441).

One way to consider the sports dilemma is that if everything goes well, if the varsity wins, if athletics stays "off the front page," the president then receives no credit, no letters of congratulations. The faculty does not pass a resolution of support or appreciation. But if the team falters, if scandal clouds the campus, if the university is embarrassed, the president almost always takes substantial blame. The faculty may pass a resolution of "no confidence" (Blackburn and Nyikos 1974). Alumni may start making telephone calls. The board may want an explanation. And the president may be looking for another job. The legitimate activities of a university and its administration can be put on hold for months while an entanglement in athletics is studied, dissected, and debated. Presidents face a serious confusion of roles in matters of athletics policy and administration (Davis 1979, pp. 425–26). Small wonder, then, that presidents usually discover that the safest action in this contentious environment is inaction, that the best thing to do with athletics is "nothing" (Hanford 1976). Beyond saying the "right thing," is it prudent to risk one's office on something as educationally peripheral as athletics? Even the most courageous college presidents find that accepting the local status quo is the best strategy. Even faculty who push for presidential intervention in athletics (if no place else) may be better served by presidents who do not sacrifice themselves tilting at athletic windmills.

On the other hand, upsetting the status quo can rudely introduce a new president to the prevailing campus athletics ethos. In 1988, for example, first-year Indiana University President Thomas Ehrlich committed a cardinal Hoosier sin when he openly criticized popular, successful basketball coach Bobby Knight. Not only did the incident make the front page locally; it also was featured on every sports page in America. Although Indiana faculty strongly supported their new president's stance, a Bloomington secretary expressed popular opinion when she complained to a *USA Today* reporter, "At the next rally, we're going to get rid of the president" (quoted in Weir 1988). Coach Knight talked of going to the University of New Mexico, kindled by a personal invitation from the governor of New Mexico. Meanwhile, President Ehrlich talked of "patching things up," reinforcing a basic research finding: When a president deals with college sports, three things can happen, and two of them are bad. Perhaps even this view is too optimistic, as one president of a university in Texas explained, "For a college president, big-time athletics is hell. For every one good thing that happens, nine bad things happen." No wonder some college and university presidents view intercollegiate athletics "much in the same light as they would regard the illegitimate son at a family reunion" (Nelson 1982, p. 55).

The modern university is complex yet fragile. Its many constituent groups compete for attention, power, money, and the president's time. A major university president's calendar is never empty, leaving him with more to do and less power than in earlier periods. Thus, many presidents have shifted from internal academic concerns to external activities like fund raising, public relations, and legislative affairs (Kerr 1984). Big-time college athletics has also shifted from an internal activity to an external extravaganza driven more by priorities of public relations than by concern about education and students (Sack 1982, pp. 80–85). External presidents and external athletics are perhaps the most visible university symbols—and a winning symbol is preferable to a losing one. A winning team may afford the president leverage (or at least freedom) to press forward on other academically important fronts. This schizoid nature of college sports (Sack 1982, pp. 80–89) leaves several questions: What do presidents do? What should their roles be? Can presidents make a difference in intercollegiate athletics? (American Council on Education 1979; Davis 1979, p. 421).

The Prescribed Presidential Role

In the beginning, athletics had no "presidential role." Sporting events were run by students because "the faculty and administrators in early colleges and universities never planned anything as frivolous as sports and games as part of the curriculum" (Davenport 1985, p. 6). As athletic contests between rival colleges became popular, however, presidents were quick to appreciate the benefits of publicity. In 1893, 40,000 spectators attended the Princeton-Yale game in New York City (Rudolph 1962, p. 375). Then as now faculty were alert to sports' "curse of bigness" and misplaced priorities. At the nation's second oldest college, for example, a faculty committee was formed to oversee student athletics, "entrusted with the general oversight of field and track athletes, and . . . authorized to forbid any features of these exercises [that] endanger the health or morals of the participants" (College of William and Mary catalog 1895). At the same time, athletics associations led by alumni became a popular organizational form. By the turn of the century, the struggle for control of athletics was under way:

> *Faculty had difficulty gaining control of the athletic associations. At the time athletic departments were forming, college presidents were in tune with the materialism and took the approach that athletics advertised the university and directly correlated with increased enrollment. College presidents became active marketing agents for athletics, attending games, speaking to victorious teams, and soliciting funds from alumni and boards of trustees, while institutions began to provide money for teams, absorb their debts, and grant scholarships. College presidents often sided with the development of athletics rather than with the faculty* (Gilley and Hickey 1986, p. 19).

At the same time this internal contest for control was taking place within each campus, another larger game was being played over the heads of most faculty and presidents: The NCAA was evolving as the governing body (Lawrence 1987b, pp. 1–37).

Controlling College Sports:
An NCAA Primer

Although several governing bodies control intercollegiate athletics (e.g., the National Association of Intercollegiate Athletics, the National Junior College Athletic Association, the Little College Athletic Association), the National Collegiate Athletic Association is the major organizational player in college sports. Founded early in the 20th century, the NCAA now has about 1,000 members: colleges and universities, athletics conferences, and coaches' associations.

As of June 1989, the 797 member colleges and universities of the NCAA were divided into three divisions according to philosophy regarding, size of, and expenditures for intercollegiate athletics. Division I, with 293 members, is home to major college sports. Division I universities must offer at least six sports for men (or for men and women) and six for women. They may offer grants-in-aid to athletes without regard to students' financial need, but the number of grants given in each sport is determined by the NCAA's limits and institutional resources and priorities.

Division I is further subdivided into Divisions I-A and I-AA, a distinction urged by major football powers and created to separate the truly big-time football programs (I-A) from the other Division I schools. Division I-A schools must offer seven sports each for men and for women and must meet other criteria for their football programs (e.g., size of stadium, attendance, schedule). Division I-A includes 105 schools with major football programs; Division I-AA has 89 with smaller football programs (that is, fewer grants-in-aid permitted for that one sport). Ninety-nine other Division I schools have no football program or field football teams in the less competitive Division II or III. These so-called I-AAA schools tend to be schools with major basketball programs that have opted out of a major involvement in football.

Division II has 191 and Division III 313 schools. Institutions in both divisions must sponsor at least four men's and four women's sports. Division II schools *may* offer grants-in-aids to student-athletes. In what philosophically is probably the major distinction among NCAA divisions, Division III schools are not permitted to offer scholarships to athletes not based on need. Division III, with the largest number of members among NCAA divisions, represents sports in small colleges.

Each year the NCAA issues a new edition of its *Manual* (latest one 1989–90), including the constitution, operating and administrative bylaws, and a section on administrative organization. (A major project to rewrite the *Manual* shortened the 1989–90 edition to 399 pages!) NCAA rules, as stated in the *Manual,* vest control of intercollegiate athletics in individual member institutions and their conferences, with each institution having the option of "administrative control or faculty control, or a combination of the two" (NCAA 1989, Art. 6.01.1; cf. Tow 1982, pp. 113–14). Left unsaid, however, is that an institution's board also may have some vested interest in this balance of power back home. On paper, at least, college presidents control the NCAA because they control the vote: "Delegates shall be certified to the NCAA national office as entitled to represent the member in question by the proper executive officers of their institutions or organizations" (NCAA 1989, Art. 5.1.2.4(a)).

But "this assertion has no substance in the practical world" (Bok 1985, p. 210), because presidents are too busy to keep abreast of excessive details that constitute the NCAA's deliberations. True control of the NCAA rests with athletics directors and the single faculty representative allowed each member institution. (Indeed, the *perceived* lack of effective presidential authority led recently to formation of the Presidents Commission within the NCAA, discussed later.) Presidential control of intercollegiate athletics is mandated not only by the NCAA but also by regional accrediting agencies: For example, "the administration and faculty of the institution must have control of the athletic program and contribute to its ultimate direction with appropriate participation by students and governing boards" (Southern Association of Colleges and Schools 1984, Sec. 5.5.2.9). And the executive directors of the regional accrediting associations' commission endorsed the principle:

While organizational details such as status of coaches and athletic directors will vary with local conditions, ultimate responsibility for all programs rests with the chief executive officer of the institution and the governing board. In the institutional governance structure, the committee overseeing athletic programs should involve representatives of appropriate constituencies, including administrators, faculty, and students (quoted in NCAA 1981, pp. iii–iv).

Even the NCAA itself suggests that institutional self-study should emphasize the president's or chancellor's role. Member institutions are asked to consider a question—"While certain authority may be delegated, does the CEO insist upon the proper conduct of the athletics program in all of its aspects?"—followed by an article of self-examination: "Does the CEO insist that athletes be subject to a strict code of ethics . . . and that deliberate and conscious violation of that code will result in severe consequences?" (NCAA 1981, pp. 9–10). Institutions' own rules, regulations, faculty handbooks, board statements, and other official documents attest to the president's ultimate authority and responsibility. Some college catalogs follow the example of Princeton University's 1986–87 *Undergraduate Announcements* with a clear statement that "academic authorities should control athletics." All of which suggests a syllogism: Presidents are ultimately responsible for college sports. Things are not right in college sports. Does it follow, then, that presidents are to blame?

The NCAA Presidents Commission

After years of sports scandals, a group of concerned university presidents began to meet in the early 1980s under the auspices of the American Council on Education (ACE) to consider issues and actions (Bok 1985). One of their most important decisions was to work within the system rather than to attempt external reform. That is, they tried to change NCAA rules from within rather than to act as mavericks who circumvented the national organization. It probably was a wise tactical decision, because the presidents protected themselves from being branded as out-of-touch zealots set on dismantling intercollegiate athletics. Further, proposed reforms would likely come about more quickly within a modified existing structure than if a wholly new organization were formed. Merely debating the shape of a new structure would have consumed years.

Their proposal was to create a board of presidents within the NCAA, vesting it with broad powers over organizational functions. The rationale was that presidents are far too busy to stay on top of the notoriously arcane details of athletic issues; therefore, a group selected by peers would be entrusted to spend time understanding issues and "do the right thing" for all. Such a board would have some control of the NCAA's agenda. ACE and the presidents lobbied intensely for adoption of their proposal at the NCAA annual convention in January 1984. Many observers thought the effort represented the presidents' final good-faith attempt to work within the NCAA. The presidents also lobbied for a series of recommendations and rules changes in two specific areas: minimal academic criteria for freshmen's participation and satisfactory performance in courses for student-athletes who wished to remain eligible. The NCAA convention, worried about its tarnished image, adopted a "get tough" mood and overwhelmingly approved regulations on these latter specific concerns. Opposition did develop, however, on the matter of establishing a board of presidents.

The NCAA staff presented its own counterproposal: creation of the Presidents Commission, with less power than the ACE's proposed board. It was seen as a "cut-'em-off-at-the-pass" tactic that would give the presidents a hollow victory. NCAA leaders sensed a convention ready to encourage more presidential involvement and control, however, and the Presidents Commission was created at the 1984 convention. It was a hybrid that was less powerful than the presidents had sought yet more representative than the NCAA staff perhaps desired. The commission, described in Article 4.5 of the NCAA's constitution, is comprised of 44 members elected by their peers. Twenty-two are from Division I institutions, 11 from Division II, and 11 from Division III. The weighted composition of the commission indicates that problems in athletics are viewed primarily as problems of big-time programs; that is, although the NCAA has more Division III institutions than Division I institutions (313 to 293), Division I presidents hold twice as many seats on the commission than the numerically superior Division III institutions. Presidents vote for members only within their own division. Terms are four years, limited to two terms, and the commission elects its own chair. The Presidents Commission is empowered to do several things:

1. Review any activity of the association;
2. Place any matter of concern on the agenda for any meeting of the council for any NCAA convention;

3. Commission studies of intercollegiate athletics and urge certain courses of action;
4. Propose legislation directly to the convention;
5. Establish the final sequence of legislative proposals in any convention agenda, within the provisions of Section 2-(e) of the Special Rules of Order;
6. Call for a special meeting of the association under provisions of Article 5.7 of the constitution;
7. Designate, before printing notice of any convention, specific proposals for which a roll-call vote of eligible voters will be mandatory;
8. Approve appointment of an executive director of the association (NCAA 1989).

Critical review suggests that only four of the eight powers significantly changed existing arrangements—and two of them had been approved before creation of the commission in 1984. The substantial gain in item 3 is that for the first time, presidents have access to the NCAA's substantial budget to support studies they want. Not coincidentally, the commission acquired power of approval for an executive director (item 8) the same year a new executive director was named. The two most important provisions are item 5 and, in particular, item 7. The convention votes on proposals in sequence, often more than 100 of them and many accompanied by extensive floor debate and lasting several days. Final proposals that fail to come for consideration before adjournment are not considered until a later meeting, which could mean a year's delay. Voting delegates often are tired and impatient toward the end of the meeting. Because an important tactic is for significant proposals to be presented early in the proceedings, the Presidents Commission gains great leverage with its power to set the order of consideration.

At the same time, the right to call for roll-call votes puts athletics directors and faculty representatives on record so that presidents know how their appointed representatives actually voted. When a president directs that a certain vote be cast, he can now be certain that it was. Yet this power also is a double-edged sword because on sensitive issues presidents themselves can no longer hide behind a secret ballot. Diverse constituents at home will know where the president stood.

Creation of the NCAA Presidents Commission and adoption

of tougher rules for eligibility at the 1984 convention brought great praise (and expectations) from presidents and the nationwide press. Even cynics believed the NCAA finally was getting serious about reform. But subsequent reform has not come easily (Lederman 1987a). Initial agreement and a heady sense of progress soon turned to disagreement and stagnation. Presidents did not necessarily agree among themselves about what needed fixing (Lederman 1987b). In summer 1987, the commission issued an "agenda for reform," with three direct questions: how to maintain integrity, how to contain costs and balance athletics and other programs, and how to define the proper role of athletics in American higher education.* The published agenda was followed by a special NCAA convention in Dallas to address issues of containing costs. The reforming presidents were soundly thrashed; their proposals to contain costs were defeated. Editorial opinion across the country indicated that athletics directors, not presidents, were back in control of the NCAA. Reform had been put on hold.

John Slaughter, then chancellor of the University of Maryland and chair of the Presidents Commission (and also embroiled in problems with athletics on his own campus), suggested that the presidents had not lobbied sufficiently hard, submerging themselves instead in fine details about athletics. Florida State University Athletics Director C.W. Ingram echoed the sense of presidential micromanagement: "I'm not against presidents' getting involved, but I don't think presidents have enough time to spend on athletics to take the role they're in" (quoted in Farrell 1987, p. 1). A general rule is that athletics directors do not think presidents know enough about intercollegiate athletics to manage them (Frey 1985). And, as a general rule, presidents agree (cf. American Council on Education 1979, pp. 349–50; Miller 1982, pp. 92–93).

In September 1987, *The Chronicle of Higher Education* proclaimed that a "rift among presidents perils [the] drive to reform big-time college sports" (Lederman 1987b). Ira Michael Heyman, a leading reformer and chancellor of the University of California at Berkeley, called for more studies and data, believing the debate was being based on anecdote, not fact. Others countered that sufficient data were available but that problems were obvious and prompt action needed. Perhaps the view of most Division I presidents was best

*NCAA Presidents Commission 3 June 1987, correspondence.

expressed by Colorado's E. Gordon Gee: "If there was a will that could be imposed, it would have occurred already" (quoted in Lederman 1987b). A year later at a special NCAA meeting in Orlando, presidents, athletics directors, coaches, and faculty representatives were talking again. Although no resolutions were passed, they sought common ground. Congressman Tom McMillen of Maryland, a former Rhodes scholar and star basketball player at the University of Maryland and on a professional team, told the gathering, "The NCAA is at a crossroads and the question today is, 'Will you get back to your original mission of educating young people?' If you do not accept that mission, others will require that it be done" (quoted in Lederman 1988a). Threat of government intervention always gets attention, as it was the stimulus to create the NCAA over 80 years ago. Failure of colleges and universities to act themselves has opened the door for relegating oversight to "others" and for the legal regulation of sports (Gerber 1979).

The Presidents Commission certainly has brought attention to problems in athletics and has reasserted the necessity of presidential leadership. Yet *some* presidents think (or, publicly say) that matters are all right, that athletics are not overemphasized and are not an especially high priority for presidential attention, and that all that is needed is fine tuning (see, e.g., Gilley and Hickey 1986, pp. 3–7). For presidents and researchers, however, the problem calls for more than changes in rules and enforcement (Frey 1982; Hanford 1976; Rooney 1987). The task is no less than establishing a proper balance between academics and athletics in the university, which is clearly a question of academic integrity. Why then are such "solutions" as the Presidents Commission not working well? (Rooney 1987, pp. xvii–xix). If "all politics is local politics," the explanation may be found by analyzing presidential leadership on the home campus. Presidents usually find agreement on athletics easier among fellow presidents, off campus. A logical proposal for reform at the president's club meets more resistance when a lone president presents it to a room full of campus athletics boosters. Even Chancellor Heyman reassured his California Golden Bear supporters, "For all my California friends, . . . I want you to know that I do not embrace unilateral disarmament in athletics, although I would welcome multilateral deemphasis" (Heyman 1987b).

Problems of Presidential Leadership

No doubt the most serious problems in college athletics occur at the big-time sports institutions—most of which are large, complex organizations. "The more intense, the more visible, and the more costly the athletic program, the less influence the chief executive officer has over it" (Atwell 1979, p. 367). The apparent lack of presidential control in big-time sports may, in part, be a function of a general dilution of presidential authority in large universities (Davis 1979, pp. 425–27; Nelson 1982, pp. 52–56; Nyquist 1979, pp. 377–78). Perhaps the many campus constituencies simply expect too much of presidents. Steven Muller, president of Johns Hopkins, asks about today's university presidents: "If it is true that none among us has attained the dominant stature, the mantle of national advocacy, why is this so?" He goes on to say, "The finest of our predecessors rose to an opportunity that may no longer exist for those of us who hold university presidencies today. . . . There may be no great university presidents today. But there are great universities, greater than yesterday's. And the men and women who captain them are no unworthy breed" (Muller 1987, p. 705).

The harsh news is that abuses in intercollegiate athletics will be solved only when presidents and institutions act in concert.

This point is intriguing because the president of a contemporary research university is faced with leading an enormous, complex institution characterized by multiple priorities and opinions (Kerr 1963). And therein lies a partial answer to the question of why big-time sports resist reform. University presidents are so consumed by their own institutional issues that few have time for problems that can be solved only by widespread cooperation *among* institutions. A truism in college sports is that no one president or institution will make a dramatic move *alone*. Not even a courageous president will dare to embrace the notion of "unilateral disarmament." The harsh news is that abuses in intercollegiate athletics will be solved only when presidents and institutions act in concert.

Review of recent studies (American Council on Education 1979; Gilley and Hickey 1986) suggests that until more university presidents adopt a wide, rather than a parochial, view of their responsibilities, little conscious reform will happen. Individual presidents make a difference for the whole of higher education only when they speak out and act decisively on issues significant to all (see, e.g., Atwell 1979, pp. 372–73). A few specific cases illustrate the point that in college sports reform, individual presidents have made a difference.

For example, the director of the Center for the Study of Sport in Society at Northeastern University offered the following projection:

> *The exit of John B. Slaughter, former chancellor of the University of Maryland, and I. Michael Heyman, chancellor of the University of California at Berkeley, from the National Collegiate Athletic Association Presidents Commission will lead to a decline in leadership in college athletics at the CEO level. The decline in that leadership, which had been going on since the creation of the commission in 1984, will mean a reversal in terms of decision making, with athletic directors again assuming command. This will be unfortunate, because many problems in college athletics can be traced to the fact that many athletics programs have operated separately from institutions, with little or no accountability to the president or chancellor* (Lapchick 1987, p. 5).

The University of California at Berkeley Chancellor Heyman is an articulate critic of big-time college abuses, having addressed the NCAA annual meeting, given speeches before his own alma mater, written articles and editorials in the national press, and called for cooperation and action from his fellow presidents. His advocacy admittedly is easier than it might be for others because he is chief executive officer at one of the most academically prestigious and well-supported institutions in the world. His license to criticize sports is greater than, say, that of the president of the University of Oklahoma or even Ohio State, where expectations for football and basketball for a statewide constituency are extraordinary (see, e.g., Nelson 1982, p. 56).[1]

The 1987 special NCAA convention contained the polarities of presidential views. While Heyman was saying, "Many of us have become calloused to corruption," President Frank Horton of the University of Oklahoma was commenting, "The NCAA would be unwise, I believe, to legislate mediocrity by legislating away the possibility of excellence" (quoted in Lederman 1987a, p. 33). The upshot was that *The Chronicle of*

---

1. *At Ohio State University, for example, football coach Earl Bruce was fired even though his won-loss record was the best among incumbent Big Ten coaches. His case illustrates extraordinary expectations, often from beyond the athletics department. Important to note is that the athletics director at Ohio State resigned in protest when he learned that Bruce had been fired.*

Higher Education called Heyman a "lonely advocate of reform." The implication for research is the insight that even if Oklahoma's president agreed with Chancellor Heyman, he could not say so publicly without jeopardizing his own job, for alumni, citizens, and students at the University of Oklahoma expect a national football championship each year. And two years ago, the Sooner men's basketball team played in the NCAA championship game. The University of California at Berkeley may strive to be competitive in Division I play, but it has no such expectations for national championships in football and basketball as does Oklahoma. Neither institution is likely to change its ethos or priorities. Is it reasonable, then, to expect a president to move far beyond the constraints of campus tradition and norms? And the notion of institutional "fit" also plays a role: A university chooses as its leaders men and women who ascribe to the institutional ethos. The University of Oklahoma would not consciously choose a president who advocated the deemphasis of varsity football. By the same logic, Columbia University probably would not take seriously a presidential aspirant who pledged to take the Lions to the top of the Associated Press and United Press International polls—except perhaps in their perennially strong areas of soccer, fencing, or federal research grants!

Another constraint on reform is that presidents need cooperation from their governing boards (Oliva 1989). Take the case of University of Miami President Edward T. Foote, II, and the Miami football team. Although the Hurricanes consistently contend for—and sometimes win—the national championship in sportswriters' polls, they have been plagued by problems. Some players have been arrested, engaged in unsportsmanlike activities, failed drug tests, and done notoriously poor academic work—all of which have tarnished the university's image. The editor of the student newspaper said of the repeated offenses, "A lot of students got sick and tired of hearing about it" (Debbie Morgan, quoted in *Chronicle of Higher Education,* 30 September 1987, p. A36). Ironically, all these events took place while President Foote was working effectively to improve the institution's academic quality. He was caught in a bind, as at least one influential member of the university's governing board said that nothing would interfere with the Hurricanes's drive to be nationally competitive in football (Sullivan 1987). Foote continues to negotiate the mine field of great expectations for athletics within academe.

Certainly it is not easy. It may not even be possible, reinforcing research findings on presidential "role confusion" (Davis 1979, pp. 425–27) and institutional "cross pressures" (Miller 1982, pp. 92–93).

Another interesting case is that of former Chancellor John Slaughter of the University of Maryland at College Park. In leaving Maryland to become president of Occidental College in California, Slaughter responded to a reporter's query about whether reform of college sports was feasible with the thoughtful comment, "I don't know whether it can be done. That's probably a different answer than I would have given you a year ago, when I would have been a lot more optimistic" (Asher 1988). Presidential burnout comes with the territory.

At another extreme, those presidents who do stand up to athletic excess may now enjoy vindication—and be attractive to some universities with big-time athletics. Paul Hardin, chancellor of the University of North Carolina at Chapel Hill, for example, was fired in 1974 as president of Southern Methodist University after he exposed significant violations of NCAA rules on his own campus (Oberlander 1988c). SMU subsequently went on to great success in football—followed by unprecedented scandal and even the sanction of the NCAA's "death penalty," a two-year ban on varsity football. Hardin, in contrast, apparently presented to the Chapel Hill search committee the brand of leadership that many at North Carolina now seek. The institutional "fit" now calls for both excellence and reform in athletics, without which a candidate like Hardin probably would not have the opportunity to lead. Such are the limits of presidential power.

Presidential Leadership in an Ambiguous Setting

University presidents operate in an imprecise, ambiguous, and complex setting. They must be politicians and mediators (Kerr 1963, pp. 29–41) more than scholars or entrepreneurs.

The American college or university is a prototypic organized anarchy. It does not know what it is doing. Its goals are either vague or in dispute. Its technology is familiar but not understood. Its major participants wander in and out of the organization. These factors do not make a university a bad organization or a disorganized one, but they do make it a problem to describe, understand, and lead (Cohen and March 1974, p. 3).

In such an equivocal world, "The confusion disturbs the president, but it also serves him. Ambiguity of power leads to a parallel ambiguity of responsibility" (Cohen and March 1974, p. 198). Nowhere is this ambiguity more striking for presidential authority than in intercollegiate athletics. If no one is in charge, no one is to blame. Presidents, as well as athletics directors, may hide behind the NCAA umbrella when things turn bad. In turn, the NCAA may call for more presidential "input." The confusion over control is bothersome, but at times it can be comforting.

In the confusion and competition is a " 'kind of lawlessness' in any large university with many separate sources of initiative and power; . . . the task is to keep this lawlessness within reasonable bounds . . ." (Kerr 1982, p. 35). The potential for 'lawlessness" may be greater in the athletics department than in any other department within the university because it is more independent than the others. Its unusual autonomy derives primarily from "its ability to forge alliances with external constituencies with political and economic strength" (Frey 1985, p. 184). A partnership of powerful external boosters and the athletics department is a formidable opponent for a meddling president. This partnership makes entrepreneurial athletics directors especially strong. At some universities, the athletics director may have a better chance than the president to prevail in a major confrontation (see, e.g., Davis 1979, pp. 425–27; Miller 1982, pp. 91–94). The array of potent forces that support a strong athletics department must give any president pause when considering reform of athletics (Frey 1982, pp. 223–38).

While local power elites frustrate presidential involvement and leadership, presidents must work to forge their own coalitions with students, parents, alumni, legislators, and others to help universities temper big-time athletics programs. Substantial, though often quiet, support exists in the wider university community for reasonable standards for athletics departments. Presidents need to find and consolidate this support. And they *must* involve, inform, and persuade their governing boards that at stake is the erosion of public confidence and trust in higher education.

Repeated public scandal undoubtedly erodes public confidence. Recently a panel organized by the Council for Advancement and Support of Education (CASE) sent a letter to more than 3,000 college presidents warning that higher education could lose the American public's confidence if it did not improve itself:

Scandals in college athletics, allegations that university researchers have been involved in scientific fraud and misconduct, and attacks on higher education by political leaders have all contributed to an erosion of public confidence . . . (quoted in Palmer 1988, p. A17).

Reports note that presidents of major universities must take a more prominent leadership role for higher education (American Council on Education 1979). Although it may be true, as Johns Hopkins University President Muller says, that universities are greater today than before because presidents are tending to issues closer to home, the need is still present for wider public participation by presidents in issues that affect all of higher education. As U.S. Senator and former President of Duke University Terry Sanford said in an essay on cooperative leadership, "We need leadership in higher education to combat the growing apprehension that we do not know where we are going" (1977, p. 12). Maybe we do yearn for presidential giants with moral conviction and courage "who are dedicated enough to the purpose of higher education that they will expend themselves, if necessary, for that purpose" (Kauffman 1980, p. 114).

These concerns are moral ones, of course (Hanford 1979; Nyquist 1979). Even though the initial discussion here of institutions' athletics budgets suspended moral outrage in favor of dispassionate critical financial analysis, the criteria shift when turning to issues of institutional propriety and purpose. Hence, critical analysis of athletics policy eventually and ultimately is at least in part about institutional ethics—the complex question of what the university should be and how it perhaps can best be approached, if not fully achieved. An institution out of balance is not all it can be, and surely some major universities have lost their perspective on the athletic playing fields. It is right and proper that members of the higher education community concern themselves with moral question about universities, not merely with gate receipts and the balance sheet (cf. Blumenstyk 1989). Otherwise, universities jeopardize their societal privileges as *special* institutions. Universities must justify themselves on more than economic terms. "Universities must make themselves into moral communities because the consequences are bad and beginning to show," and they "should encourage behavior that transcends the readily acceptable" (Callahan 1988). One problem is that a university can abide by NCAA rules and still fall short of public trust if it supports football and basketball programs to the detriment of the rest of the institution. And, the NCAA clearly notes, ultimate responsibility rests with individual institutions and their conferences, not with the NCAA (Tow 1982, pp. 112–14). Excessive athletics programs corrupt our common values of balance and fair play. Protecting the integrity of colleges and universities demands active presidential involvement. We should ask, and expect, no less.

In protecting the integrity of the institution, presidents must, of course, have support from their governing boards. A philosophical dialogue about athletics must take place between presidents and boards, not merely discussions of won-loss records and attendance figures (NCAA 1981, pp. 9–10). Governing boards must seek presidents committed to balance and moderation in athletics (Oliva 1989), and if they do not, we must insist that they do. Education, not athletic success, is the primary concern of boards (Baliles, cited in Blumenstyck 1989, pp. A15).

Many critics, and presidents themselves, say that reform must begin at home. Yet the home campus is where the greatest political risk awaits a college or university president. Presidential talk of balance in athletics at a national forum may be tolerated back home, but concerted leadership or decisive action may not. Actions at home can jeopardize a president's job. Because a lonely vigil at the home campus is both risky and ineffective for a president, increased cooperation among presidents is essential for effective, proper reform, following in part from the NCAA's emphasis that the *conference* to which an institution belongs *voluntarily* is a crucial unit of self-determination (Tow 1982, pp. 112–14).

Given this organizational fact, one possibility for structural change is for college presidents to begin seriously rethinking conference affiliations. A number of presidents and athletics directors at major universities reinforce the view that any given conference contains some members who do not truly "fit." Some flaunt rules and propriety. And, to another extreme, other member institutions lag in fielding reasonably competitive teams. Athletic conferences are a prime example of voluntary association among supposedly peer institutions (Boyer

1985; Carnegie Foundation 1982). This standard ought to be periodically reexamined so that alliances in athletics are based on academic similarities and educational mission as well as expectations for athletics. By this criterion, the Ivy League comes to mind (Lederman 1986; Thelin 1976, pp. 25-34). It is demonstrated in Division III by the newly formed University Athletic Association, whose charter members include such institutions as the University of Chicago, New York University, the University of Rochester, Washington University, Case-Western Reserve, Carnegie-Mellon, and Johns Hopkins University. This group of major research universities represents a partnership "whose chief principle is that sports are part of the educational process and should be conducted in a manner consistent with an institution's academic mission" *(Chronicle of Higher Education* 2 July 1986, p. A17). In a similar spirit, the cooperative action of the presidents and athletics directors at Holy Cross, Bucknell, Colgate, Lafayette, Lehigh, and Davidson formed the new Division I-AA Colonial League (Childs 1987; Lederman 1986, p. 40).

"Traditional rivalries" and expected gate receipts, of course, stand in the way of realigning conferences. But, as noted earlier, even big-time athletics often loses money, and as for the alleged durability of traditional rivalries, times—and institutions—change (cf. Michener 1976, pp. 219-80). One impetus for forming the "Ivy Group" was the collective concern of several presidents about the University of Pennsylvania's emphasis on football teams of national caliber (Thelin 1976, pp. 30-33). The Princeton-Rutgers football games illustrate how changing institutional priorities alter traditional sports rivalries. In 1869, the two teams played the first intercollegiate game in the United States and off and on for over a century maintained an in-state rivalry. Both are historic, pre–Revolutionary War universities as well as nearby neighbors in New Jersey. But as Rutgers developed an increasing appetite (as yet unfulfilled) for national prominence in athletics, the long-standing series was ended. When a particular institution's values and attitudes about academics and athletics are markedly different from conferencewide norms, isolation through exclusion can be a sound policy for reform in athletics. If universities refuse to play against institutions whose actions suggest disrespect for or ignorance of the academic thread that holds conferences and rivalries together, policies and practices will change. Such was the impetus for creation of the Ivy League over 30 years ago. Now may be the time to again rethink conference alliances. Presidents and boards of trustees would do well to have conferences whose members genuinely share academic mission and moderation in athletics, not merely a fierce football rivalry (cf. NCAA 1981, pp. 7–8). And presidents can start the dialogue. "Everything starts at the institutional level and it starts with the committed leadership of the CEO, supported by the governing board. Because athletic disarmament, as a practical matter, can never be unilateral, there must be agreement at least within conferences" (Atwell 1988, p. 9).

This strategy is based on the research finding that presidents do make a difference in institutional direction (Kerr 1984), including intercollegiate athletics. It meshes with the tradition of self-regulation and self-determination in collegiate athletics (El-Khawas 1979). Presidents, especially presidents working together, can make a difference in policy about athletics.

The question is, will the presidents be able, in the words of one long-term distinguished president, to "take charge"? Perhaps it is too much to ask presidents to take courageous (some might say foolhardy) stands to enable their institutions to take charge of their own destinies. Perhaps that is why the NCAA with complex rules and harsher sanctions looks so good to many presidents.

On the other hand, perhaps presidents can ill afford not to take charge. In the words of legendary University of North Carolina President William Friday, "It is clear that presidents must act, must lead, must show courage unless they want national disapproval" (Gilley and Hickey 1986, p. 9).

INTERCOLLEGIATE ATHLETICS
AND INSTITUTIONAL ADMINISTRATION

Beyond the Presidential Panacea

Even though the studies and reports summarized in the preceding section indicate that college and university presidents ought play a strong leadership role in policy for intercollegiate athletics, they emphasize at the same time a seeming contradiction: The presidential role in the administration and management of college sports at the campus level should be reduced and diffused (see, e.g., American Council on Education 1979; NCAA 1981, pp. 10–12). The weakness of advocating "more presidential involvement" in the college's athletics program is that it is the same panacea suggested for virtually *every* campus problem. Presidents in recent years have been urged to become more involved with the educational life of the institution, in contrast with being primarily "external presidents" (Kerr 1984).

The cumulative result is that the president is expected to do everything and nothing. If the president is to be a true leader, his or her involvement will be most effective if it is selectively reserved for the most significant policy issues. Micromanagement is a disastrous recipe for presidential involvement with intercollegiate athletics (cf. Davis 1979, pp. 426–27). Presidents, then, need help. At the same time, one endemic problem of intercollegiate athletics departments is their isolation (Frey 1982, pp. 223–38; Massengale and Merriman 1981).

Indeed, on several campuses, the governance and control of intercollegiate athletics, particularly football and basketball, are independent of the usual lines of authority. As one university president has remarked, they are "frequently far more autonomous and unrelated to the campus than such tyrannical and cussedly independent siblings as Medicine and Law" (Nyquist 1979, p. 378).

To solve these coexisting problems, one strategy is to integrate intercollegiate athletics into the institutional fabric (Hanford 1979, pp. 363–65). This section focuses on the various characters and roles in the supporting cast: vice presidents, deans, athletics directors, staff, and faculty (Davis 1979; NCAA 1981; Nelson 1982).

Faculty Involvement

Perhaps the weakest, most curious, link in the governance of intercollegiate athletics is the faculty's role (Blackburn and

Intercollegiate athletics, the NCAA, and university presidents would be better integrated to educational mission if faculty-controlled athletics policy committees were just that—policy making.

Nyikos 1974). At major universities where signs of flagrant abuses in athletics programs have been revealed, faculty initiative in reforming college sports has been laggard, leading one observer to ask, "Where are the faculty?" (Weistart 1987, pp. 12–17). On the one hand is perennial rhetoric about "faculty control" and "faculty involvement" (Miller 1982, p. 98; NCAA 1981, pp. 12–13; Tow 1982, p. 114), but on the other, the rhetoric is usually unclear in policy statements and weak in practice (Guttmann 1982, pp. 75–76; Scott 1956, pp. 30–32). The NCAA's suggested guidelines usually combine "faculty and administration" as if the two are one and the same. In fact, at most universities the central administration—the president—has control over intercollegiate athletics, and many organizational charts completely bypass even remote faculty control. Some institutions have a faculty advisory committee—but it is *advisory*, not unlike playing basketball without keeping score, and it really does not count when authority for making decisions is at stake (cf. Frey 1982, pp. 223–38). Recent major studies on governance and control of intercollegiate athletics (American Council on Education 1979; Gilley and Hickey 1986, pp. 3–7) omit analysis or discussion of "faculty" as a collective factor but instead emphasize the roles of the president, the board, the athletics director, or vice presidents.

The NCAA's constitution states that one of the basic purposes of the association is "to maintain intercollegiate athletics as an integral part of the educational program . . ." (NCAA 1989, Art. 1.3.1). To further this admittedly noble effort, most NCAA member institutions designate a member of their faculty as the NCAA faculty athletics representative (FAR) (NCAA 1989, Art. 6.1.3). The name can be a misnomer, for not all FARs are truly "faculty." They may be full-time administrators if they hold faculty rank or even (especially at small colleges) the athletics director himself! This incongruous situation prompted the NCAA convention to adopt in January 1989 the provision that "an individual so designated after January 12, 1989, shall . . . not hold an administrative or coaching position in the athletics department" (NCAA 1989, Art. 6.1.3). Ironically, this measure had a dysfunctional dimension for faculty involvement at some Division III institutions, "where a number of bona fide professors in academic departments also serve as coaches for so-called "Olympic sports." For many institutions (especially in NCAA Divisions I and II), institutional athletics representative (IAR) might be a more accurate title than faculty athletics representative. In fact, some colleges and universities use the title institutional athletics representative.

The president or chancellor usually appoints the FAR after consultation with the athletics director and perhaps others. Therein lies part of the problem for true involvement and influence for faculty: The FAR actually is the *president's* representative to the NCAA, not the faculty's, leading to a warning of the danger of faculty members' being co-opted when they do participate in governance of college sports (Weistart 1987, p. 14). At some institutions the position holds considerable power, at others virtually none (Miller 1982, p. 98). So much variability in—and confusion about—the FAR's role recently led to a series of annual forums for FARs, beginning at the 1985 NCAA annual meeting. As partial consequence of these gatherings, the NCAA in 1987 published its handbook for FARs. The 32-page pamphlet describes qualifications for the "ideal" FAR:

> *An institution's faculty athletics representative, to have optimum effectiveness in the position, must possess certain personal and professional qualifications.*
>
> *The FAR must have the ability to deal with people in an amicable and effective manner and must find satisfaction in working with many kinds of people. He or she must have the respect and confidence of administrators, the athletics staff, the faculty, and athletes. Therefore, the FAR must have executive ability as well as the ability to get along well with other people.*
>
> *The FAR must enjoy athletics. He or she need not be a "jock" or a "gung-ho" enthusiast about the institution's intercollegiate program, but the individual must take pleasure in all aspects of that program. The FAR should attend as many contests as possible, take an interest in the welfare of the athletes and coaches, and exhibit publicly unreserved support of the institution's teams* (NCAA 1987, p. 9).

Of course, the FAR is also expected to know intimately and understand fully (and perhaps appreciate!) the 399-page NCAA *Manual.* Is it reasonable to expect that any such person exists on a campus who at the same time maintains an active faculty life? It is doubtful. Further, the NCAA's guide for evaluating intercollegiate athletics advises that the FAR ought to have "the respect and confidence of the faculty, administration, students, and athletic staff," while also taking an "active interest in the welfare and academic problems of student-athletes" (NCAA 1981, p. 12). It goes on to say, "The faculty athletics representative is in reality the NCAA's representative on campus . . ." (p. 13). The position as described is clearly untenable. In the quarrelsome world of big-time intercollegiate athletics, representing the president of the institution to the NCAA *and* at the same time representing the NCAA to the institution is considerably challenging, if not inherently contradictory. No wonder, then, that faculty who care about policy matters regarding athletics are suspicious of this arrangement.

In fact, most faculty may be unaware that one of their colleagues is an NCAA FAR. They may know that an athletics policy committee exists, and they may know the chair of that committee (who may—or may not—be the same person as the FAR), but rarely do they know that their institution has a specific faculty member whose role is to give academic perspective to athletics programs and decisions. At most colleges and universities, FARs may prefer it this way. With many of their faculty colleagues, association with the NCAA and the athletics department threatens credibility as a member of the faculty. Academic codes and faculty values dictate that NCAA business not match teaching and scholarly activity as a meaningful endeavor for a "real" faculty member. Yet at the same time, the NCAA recommends that an FAR should have an "adjusted workload" to allow for his or her athletic duties (NCAA 1981, p. 12). Understandably, most faculty representatives are tenured, long-time full professors.

In some athletic conferences, FARs meet regularly to make and enforce rules. In other conferences, FARs have virtually no collective influence. The degree to which they do make policy and enforce rules is a reflection both of how they are selected and of institutional and conference tradition. Certainly, faculty and FARs have little official control over academic advising for student-athletes, as such academic counselors usually are employed by and report to the athletics director (Miller 1982, p. 98). And on athletic matters at most large universities, no assurance exists that FARs represent broad faculty sentiment. Their faculty colleagues may in fact mistrust them. Certainly the fact that the FAR is not elected by peers but appointed by the president increases this dissonance. Many faculty and critics of excessive athletics programs believe that all FARs are by definition co-opted by the athletic bureaucracy and cannot possibly represent fairly (or effectively) the academic point of view.

This view may have some truth to it. In merely fulfilling all athletic obligations and responsibilities, an FAR can hardly be a full-time faculty member. It is a variation of Catch-22: To be a legitimate FAR requires more time away from legitimate faculty activities than any faculty member should give. The idea of a faculty member as an athletics representative is a good one but as described by the NCAA is probably impossible (cf. Guttmann 1982, pp. 75–76). FARs at major universities may develop into administrators with at least some staff, release time, and all the attendant administrative distractions (and perks) that interfere with academic work. Other faculty may consider FARs a part of the problem, not part of the solution.

The NCAA can of course point to FARs as an indication of the seriousness with which the organization invites an academic presence (NCAA 1981, p. 12). But while probably half or more of all institutions delegate their annual NCAA voting privileges to the FAR and while close to 75 percent of NCAA presidents over the past 40 years have been FARs rather than athletics directors (Byers 1987), no one seriously believes that NCAA governance is significantly influenced by faculty concerns (see, e.g., Atwell 1979, pp. 372–73; Blackburn and Nyikos 1974). The NCAA remains largely an athletics directors' world, shared with a few long-term, visible FARs and the NCAA staff.

All of this discussion is not to disparage the intended role of the FAR (after all, one of the authors served in that role), and the concept is thoughtful. But NCAA's discussions about balance between academics and athletics are shaped more by athletics directors than by FARs. "Faculty oversight has long since ceased to be effective in most institutions" (Atwell 1988, p. 9), and even if FARs were a more powerful group, they are probably not very representative of the overall faculty's point of view.

On the other hand, the campus faculty athletics policy committee may have a great deal to say about sports programs with considerable impact—and may even represent a faculty perspective on campus (El-Khawas 1979, pp. 515–17; NCAA 1981, p. 12). It depends, however, on the ethos and structure of the institution, how the policy committee is selected, and how its charge is defined (Frey 1985, pp. 179-90; Massengale and Merriman 1981, pp. 1-17). Such committees may be elected or appointed, they may or may not have students and administrators as members, and they might set policy (but usually only advise). In one case, for example, the athletics policy committee officially became the athletics policy *advisory* committee after taking a series of unappreciated positions on athletics issues. But, according to one athletics director, "A president will normally charge a faculty-controlled committee to give scope and direction to a given athletic program, and this group will generally set policy" (Miller 1982, pp. 92-93). The committee may even approve budgets, set ticket prices, and have a hand in scheduling. In other institutions, however, the committee may struggle merely to see a complete and disaggregated budget for athletics, let alone help to shape it. Again, such variations among institutions depend on campus tradition and governance.

According to one regional accreditation commission's handbook (an example hailed by the NCAA's own 1981 booklet), faculty are given broad license to be involved in governance and policy of college sports: "Intercollegiate athletics shall be organized under faculty supervision, and they must meet ethical standards as well as the prescribed regulations of the athletic conference or association of which the institution may be a member" (NCAA 1981, p. 9). In fact, at some universities with big-time athletics programs, faculty may be officially excluded from such supervisory roles. Extreme erosion of faculty involvement in intercollegiate policy regarding athletics, for example, is illustrated by an episode at an academic senate meeting at a large state university (Thelin 1978, pp. 181-83). One professor introduced discussion about the athletics foundations's new policy that tied locations for seats at games with amount of donations to the athletics program, leading to his resolution that the university's proposed use of a "voluntary" donation for allocating seats for university sporting events directly conflicts with and reflects unfavorably upon the university's fundamental academic role. At the next meeting, the senate council responded with the following recommendation:

The Governing Regulations clearly specify that the functions of the Senate include only matters that are pertinent to aca-

demic issues. . . . We believe that this policy of restraint
should be maintained and we do not believe that the pro-
posed resolution deals with a topic that is within the scope
of traditional and proper Senate concerns (quoted in
Thelin 1978, p. 182).

The case was closed, victim of strict constructionism and
a course of logic that removed faculty from the opportunity
and responsibility to monitor the educational mission of institutional programs and resources. The case is interesting
because it signaled that at some institutions intercollegiate
athletics may not even have to go through the *ritual* or for-
malities of deference to educational purposes. Such situations
leave little surprise that faculty often tend to see themselves
as far removed from discussions about intercollegiate athletics
policy, let alone decisions (Blackburn and Nyikos 1974). From
time to time, dormant faculty involvement ends, as faculty
themselves resurrect existing machinery of governance to raise
substantive questions about policy regarding athletics. This
faculty initiative toward internal review appears to be the case
at the University of North Carolina at Chapel Hill. In spring
1988, widespread faculty concern over excesses and abuses
in varsity sports led the faculty council to vote unanimously
to investigate the role of intercollegiate athletics on campus
(Oberlander 1988b).

Intercollegiate athletics, the NCAA, and university presidents
would be better integrated to educational mission (Hanford
1979, pp. 363–64) if faculty-controlled athletics policy committees were just that—policy making rather than merely advisory in scope. It is an area for caution, for the manner of committee selection and reporting structure will determine the
effectiveness of either policy setting or advice giving. But presidents are better off when they share broad policy decision
making with a faculty committee (El-Khawas 1979, pp. 515–
17). If athletics is billed as integral to educational mission,
it makes good sense to significantly involve members of the
educational community.

The potential for inefficient and obstructive micromanagement should of course be understood. Managerial details of
planning, budgeting, and personnel must be left to the athletics director and staff, while broad philosophical directions
of a university's athletics program should have strong, formal
influence from academic quarters. Athletics directors should

welcome faculty participation for perspective and rationale and as protection from a narrow view that comes from always and only talking with the same circle of athletics professionals (NCAA 1981, pp. 7–13). Interaction is mutually beneficial, for it protects the faculty from comparable dangers of isolation.

The Athletics Director

The athletics director's life can be a difficult one, not only when dealing with faculty. Like the president, the director is responsible to diverse publics, both on and off campus. And, like the president, the director must be an adept fund raiser and congenial at public relations (Davis 1979, pp. 426–27; Miller 1982). Occasionally one still finds cases when a prominent coach (usually in football or basketball) is attracted to a particular university by the lure of a dual appointment as athletics director and head coach. But this dangerous concentration of roles and powers is increasingly rare and often signals an institution more concerned with emphasizing one or two sports at the expense of a balanced, equitable intercollegiate sports program. Gone are the days when a retired football coach became, by right, the athletics director. Now searches for athletics directors include as candidates business and public relations professionals as well as former athletes, alumni, and coaches. Some universities even give advanced degrees in athletics management. The athletics directorship is a complex job (NCAA 1981, pp. 10–11) overseeing many different people and groups—coaches, budget officers, sports information directors, fund raisers, and, indirectly, student-athletes. But to whom does the athletics director report (American Council on Education 1979, pp. 349–50)?

Athletics directors almost always make a strong case for reporting directly to the president (Miller 1982, pp. 92–93). Presidents often see the wisdom in that arrangement. Athletics may be the most visible activity a university offers, and no president wants an athletics director acting alone. But by allowing a formal structure in which the athletics director reports directly to the president, the president tacitly agrees that the intercollegiate athletics department is more than an academic department—more than the biology or English departments, whose chairs report to a dean (cf. Atwell 1988, p. 9). Intercollegiate athletics is even more than an entire academic school whose dean reports to the vice president for academic affairs. The reporting structure alone represents an imbalance of academics and athletics in the university (Frey 1982, pp. 226–27).

The conventional arrangement of having an athletics director report directly to the president also undermines and underuses an institution's diverse administrative expertise. It tends to short-circuit the authority of such vice presidential offices as administration and finance in budgeting matters. It isolates athletics programs from the umbrella of university public relations and fund raising under the auspices of the vice president for university advancement. "Rarely are athletic fund-raising efforts tied to the larger developmental operation of the university. Athletic administrators see a great deal of difficulty in bringing these groups under internal control" (Frey 1982, p. 226). Separation also tends to remove athletics from general education (Scott 1956, pp. 29–31) or from the office of student affairs (cf. Fischer 1975). Athletics directors will always have access to their presidents, no matter the formal reporting structure, but alternatives exist to the usual scheme warranting consideration.

EDUCATIONAL MISSION, ACADEMIC STRUCTURE, AND INTERCOLLEGIATE ATHLETICS POLICY: Recommendations for Reform

Structural Models and Institutional Mission

To save the president for the most important matters involving intercollegiate athletics, then, colleges and universities might consider some structural arrangements that break from the practice of having the athletics director report directly to the president (cf. Gilley and Hickey 1986, pp. 4–9). Or if one wishes to have the athletics director report directly to the president, intercollegiate athletics should be elevated to a commensurate stature within the *mission* and *structure* of the institution (Hanford 1979, pp. 363–66). This recommendation avoids some predictable problems while at the same time introducing some decidedly positive changes in academic governance.

The structural plan an institution adopts depends on how it redefines and clarifies college sports as part of its educational mission. An important ground rule is that the administrative structure and lines of authority ought to clearly and accurately reflect how an institution describes the purposes of intercollegiate athletics, a practice recommended by the NCAA to its member institutions (1981, pp. iv, 7–13).

A major aim of institutional structural reform is to enable the president to devote more attention to collaborating with presidents from other colleges and universities to deal with significant *collective* policy issues. One immediate item for collective attention by college and university presidents is the issue of rising expenses for varsity athletics programs. This problem is common to all levels of intercollegiate sports. Institutions, either at the NCAA or conference unit, should mutually agree to practices that reduce costs and at the same time nudge college sports toward congruence with sound educational priorities. For example, athletic grants-in-aid ought be awarded only on the basis of a student-athlete's financial need. A second immediate recommendation is that presidents agree to reduce the number of allowable athletic grants-in-aid below the NCAA's 1989 regulations.

For all institutions, the authors recommend dissolution of the separate athletics foundations that are legally incorporated, with their own boards. This recommendation follows the recent examples of the University of Illinois and Virginia Tech, where such foundations were dissolved in 1988. The separate

If athletics indeed is central to an institution's image and character, why not have penalties for violations accrue to the entire institution?

foundation—a private corporation within or attached to the host university—provides great temptation for a program's autonomy outside the president and the university board. The president and the board of trustees should have assurances that they, not the foundation board, are the ones to whom the athletics department must be accountable. Many athletics/educational foundations and/or booster clubs have a provision that the university president also be president of the group's board (see, e.g., Miller 1981, p. 51), but no compelling historical evidence suggests that such arrangements ensure integration into the institution's educational mission and environment. Certainly they preclude direct faculty supervision or control. To the contrary, nonprofit athletics/educational foundations and booster clubs have tended recently to move intercollegiate athletics increasingly away from academic and educational concerns (Frey 1982, pp. 223–38).

Furthermore, the athletics director often is put in the situation of reporting to two groups—the foundation's board and the university's central administration (Frey 1982, pp. 227–28). Opportunities for split allegiances, conflicting signals, and the building of fiefdoms are so great they render intercollegiate athletics unaccountable to the university itself.

Beyond this universal change, modifications of administrative structure can be tailored to put intercollegiate athletics in harmony with regional accreditation standards and with the institution's self-determined educational mission statement. The caveat is that an intercollegiate athletics program would have to identify clearly its athletics program's most dominant characteristic. Is it a central feature of university life that is an end in itself? Is it commercial? symbolic? extracurricular? educational? By focusing on one primary personality for intercollegiate athletics, a university would eliminate varsity sports from the temptation of the so-called "chameleon syndrome" (Thelin 1986), in which a program conveniently shifts its identity to match the particular circumstances of the moment. For example, even though research reports and testimonials document the "business" nature of big-time intercollegiate sports, fund raisers for athletics tend to be inconsistent in depicting their priorities and roles. One athletics official told fund raisers at a conference, "We're not in professional sports; we're in education. We are supposed to train young people for life. If we miss out on this, we've missed out on the greatest cause of all, and we've lost the big game all in one shot" (Rice 1981, p. 11). This statement of educational role coexists with markedly different statements of professional purpose and activity. At the same conference, another university's associate athletics director for financial affairs cited the following passage from an article in the *Washington Post:*

> *Red ink does not produce national championships. Thus, the fund raiser who produced the dollar is just as important as the coach who recruits the studs. Without his money, the coach wouldn't be able to afford the studs. Even worse, the school probably wouldn't be able to afford a coach capable of recruiting the studs* (Finstein, quoted in Bennett 1981, pp. 2–3).

For the associate athletics director for financial affairs addressing his professional colleagues, this passage captured the essence of what needs to be done in fund raising for athletics (Bennett 1981). Such self-depiction suggests a need to bring athletics fund raising under close academic and educational control. The following models for reorganization are presented toward that end.

- *The major mission model:* At some universities, careful self-study might lead to the finding that external constituencies and internal authorities regard big-time intercollegiate athletics as a central purpose of the institution. If so, the position of athletics director should be changed to the office of vice president for intercollegiate athletics. The varsity sports program would be sufficiently important unto itself that it would not have to justify its existence as a corollary to, say, enriching student life or providing intangible benefits to the institution. Athletics becomes comparable to research, teaching, or agricultural extension, for example—a basic function of the campus (Thelin 1982). At this level it makes good sense to have the athletics director be a vice president, reporting directly to the president. The tradeoff is that the institution would have to be committed to supporting sports in an enduring manner, not subject to vacillations in popular interest. Above all, it would make for interesting, substantive revisions of charters and mission statements central to the American tradition of institutional self-determination (El-

Khawas 1979, p. 512).

- *The commercial model:* For those universities that opt for a big-time, revenue-producing varsity sports program, two possibilities might reflect such a program. One is to have intercollegiate athletics defined as a wholly distinct auxiliary enterprise, played by student-athletes who only incidentally represent the entire student body. Athletics would thus be a unit wholly separate from, for example, academic affairs and student affairs. The athletics director would report to the vice president for financial affairs (see, e.g., Lawrence 1987b; Rooney 1987).

- *The symbolic model:* The second possibility and another variation on this theme is an institution's emphasizing the *symbolic* importance of college sports as a source of internal cohesion and external relations. Under this rubric, one could justify massive university deficits in running an athletics department because the color, the visibility, and the "intangibles" are worthwhile. The logical administrative home, then, for intercollegiate athletics would be the office of university advancement, with the athletics director reporting to the vice president responsible for fund raising, development, and external relations. Policy decisions about athletics would have to be examined and justified in terms of the function of university relations and tied to other ceremonial events and colorful rituals, such as commencement, centennial celebrations, and charter day. And because a conspicuous athletics program has an alleged benefit for the total institution, this model might employ a plan for internal taxation: All donations explicitly made for intercollegiate athletics would be subject to a substantial charge for institutional overhead. The gain for the athletics department, of course, is that a sports program that spent a lot of money and did not raise a surplus would be entitled to have its deficits absorbed by the office of university advancement—so long as that office and the vice president were persuaded that the intangible and symbolic benefits of sports warranted such subsidy.

- *The subsidy model:* Related to the symbolic model is the notion of "subsidy." A recent proposal to the Maryland state legislature, for example, recommends that the University of Maryland's intercollegiate athletics program receive direct state appropriations as part of the regular institutional budget. This proposal comes at a time when fund raising and game revenues have failed to cover varsity sports expenses. One ostensible gain is that it alleviates the pressure of varsity programs to "make money." The weakness of this proposal is the uncertainty of its connection to governance. Some support the idea on the grounds that "athletics departments should be tied to a university's budget, if only to spur debate on the role of athletics on campus," for making athletics compete with academic courses for funds could "prompt considerable dialogue about the priorities of athletics" (Atwell, cited in Sell and Goldstein 1989). The implication is that such a measure might require varsity athletics to join with academic departments in going through the regular university budgeting process.

The risk associated with this approach is that it includes no assurance that intercollegiate athletics would in fact be subject to the same procedures, pool of resources, or requirements for reporting of an academic department. If, for example, the athletics director reported directly to the president, the intercollegiate athletics department could be allowed its own distinct budget requests quite apart from, say, departments of chemistry or English. It differs from the academic model discussed later in that it does not preclude a varsity sports program from retaining the expensive features of a big-time revenue producer, including student grants-in-aid, large stadia, booster clubs, and all the other accoutrements.

- *The extracurricular model:* According to this scheme, college sports is an important part of college life but is distinct from the formal studies and academic affairs of the curriculum. If athletes indeed represent the student body, college sports might be depicted as an important activity in student life. Hence, the athletics director reports to the dean of student affairs or to the vice president for student life. Doing so tends to approximate the current scheme as portrayed in regional accreditation handbooks. And it probably comes close to approximating existing practices at many Division II and Division III institutions. It does not, however, accurately describe the locus or character of most Division I-A or I-AA intercollegiate athletics programs, where most varsity athletes receive grants-in-aid. A good example of how this model has become part of public policy and institutional policy comes from the state of Washington (Fischer 1975). Each institution is presented with the option of receiving state appropriations for varsity athletics by housing those teams under general student affairs, with the important requirement that no varsity athletes for those teams receive grants-in-aid.

- *The academic model:* A recurrent theme stated by coaches and athletics directors is that a major feature of college sports is their *educational* value. Sports build character, teach teamwork, and transmit highly desirable attitudes and values to student-athletes. Other variations on this theme include a coach's claim that he or she gains most satisfaction from watching a student-athlete receive a bachelor's degree. Closely related is the idea that athletic grants-in-aid provide a fine vehicle for social and educational mobility, making possible a college education that otherwise would be unaffordable to a young man or woman.

According to this liturgy, the varsity sports program is integral to the educational life of the institutions—an educationally proper and laudable aim. At the same time, why does one need large crowds and television audiences to witness the educational development of a small number of student-athletes? And, if the stadium or basketball arena is analogous to the laboratory or classroom, serious questions can be raised about per capita costs, not to mention cost-benefit ratios. The best way to answer such educational questions then is to make college sports part of academic affairs. In terms of the university's structure, the athletics director would thus report to the provost or to the vice president for academic affairs. Decisions about athletics programs would have to be made in concert with all other decisions about the curriculum, educational programs, and academic matters. This integration into academic affairs means that an athletics director would have to present and discuss varsity sports at the same table as the dean of the school of education or the chair of the chemistry department, for example.

This arrangement has some side benefits. One is that it breaks down the isolation of athletes from students. The second is that it promotes more interaction—and, one hopes, more understanding and cooperation among faculty and the staff of the athletics department. It would make sense for those coaches who also hold teaching appointments in physical education. It would bring questions about admissions and academic standards to the table for all categories of special admission, whether athletics or theater arts. Above all, it has the prospect of restoring faculty involvement in and access to policy about athletics. One persistent lament of athletics directors and coaches is that they do not have the support or understanding of faculty: If only professors understood the good work athletics officials are doing for student-athletes, they would be more supportive. Here is an arrangement that would promote such integration. And, as noted earlier, it is in the battle of the budget that institutions most clearly express their educational priorities in terms that count.

From Mission Statements to
Self-Study and Accountability

Changes in internal administrative structure can be enhanced only if they are tied to matters of institutional accountability (Grant 1979). One irony of the years of college sports scandals is that apparently in no case has a college or university suffered institutionwide or educational penalty for its athletic abuses. The NCAA, for example, may have barred Southern Methodist University from fielding a varsity football team for two years, but the authors know of no public reports that the *overall* standing of the institution was under review as a result of this major violation. A few years ago, improprieties in the varsity basketball program at Tulane University led the president and board to eliminate varsity basketball, even though violations in admissions, recruitment, financial aid, student housing, and course enrollments were at least indirectly part of the episode. Serious as the situation was at Tulane, nothing indicates campuswide censure. Similarly, at some colleges scandals have involved systematic alteration of student-athletes' transcripts, yet, although such cases damage the academic and administrative character of the whole institution, few signs of institutionwide overhaul exist. Internal reform of athletics usually focuses on the particular incident.

The usual practice, then, is for violations in athletics to result in penalties in athletics. If athletics indeed is central to an institution's image and character, why not have penalties for violations accrue to the entire institution? This solution is analogous to the situation with federal research grants: Violating codes can cause the halt of all federal funds to a university. The same policy is often true with regard to equal opportunity in race or gender: An institution's failure to comply in one program endangers the entire institution. Title IX legislation involving educational opportunity regardless of gender probably provides the closest approximation of this model. Thus, policies acquire clout in shaping higher education. If presidents and boards are truly serious about reform, why not implement the same policy for athletics?

A fair way to do so is to amend accreditation standards drafted by regional accrediting agencies, following from the observation that "intercollegiate athletics programs should be included in the normal accreditation process of universities to ensure that they uphold the educational mission" (Grant 1979, p. 419). First, intercollegiate athletics should be made the object of a distinct "standard"—just as in recent years the library, the computing facilities, or continuing education have been added as major entities. Second, intercollegiate athletics would no longer be included as one of many dimensions of "student life" in the 10-year review. For example, in the 1977 Standards of the Southern Association's Commission on Colleges, "athletics" is listed as number 10 of 10 items under "Standard Seven: Student Development Services." And it underscrutinizes big-time varsity sports, as it devotes two brief paragraphs that tend to link markedly different programs, noting that "intercollegiate and intramural programs should contribute to the total personal development of the student."

The concise language of the Southern Association's item on athletics is good—but its place as a single item seems to obscure the importance and dominance that intercollegiate athletics has come to occupy at many colleges and universities. Thus, the recommendation to draw out "intercollegiate athletics" as an activity worthy of its own accreditation standard fulfills the letter and spirit of some existing regional accreditation language. For example:

> *Each institution should clearly define its purpose and should incorporate this definition into a statement [that] is a pronouncement of its role in the educational world. The institution's integrity is measured not only in terms of its stated purpose, but also in terms of its conscientious endeavor to fulfill this purpose* (Southern Association 1977, p. 1).

The NCAA's guide on evaluating intercollegiate athletics programs (1981) endorses the Southern Association's language and goes on to suggest that NCAA member institutions consider the model statement drafted by the Middle States Association of Colleges and Secondary Schools in 1953:

> *The purpose of the athletic program should be clearly stated in the institution's publications and should be consonant with the purposes and objectives of higher education as a whole. . . . The statement of purposes should have been prepared with the cooperation and assistance of the faculty and administration. Actual practice and conduct of athletics programs, of course, should conform with the announced purposes* (p. 7).

Finally, the NCAA brings attention to the 1979 Massachusetts State College Athletic Conference's guidelines on the self-study of intercollegiate athletics: "An institution's Philosophy of Intercollegiate Athletics is an official statement about the Institution's intercollegiate athletics program in the context of the institution's purpose, values, and other programs and activities" (quoted in NCAA 1981, p. 7).

The Old College Try: Balancing
Academics and Athletics in Higher Education

Having sharpened the instruments and refined the mechanisms of institutional self-study, presidents in concert with faculty, deans, athletics directors, and board members—and in cooperation with counterparts at other institutions—can now be in a good position to make policies for intercollegiate athletics congruent with practice, to make college sports harmonious with the institution's distinctive self-identity and mission statement. Used well and wisely, they can promote effectiveness in the "old college try" to balance academics and athletics in higher education.

REFERENCES

The Educational Resources Information Center (ERIC) Clearinghouse
on Higher Education abstracts and indexes the current literature on
higher education for inclusion in ERIC's data base and announce-
ment in ERIC's monthly bibliographic journal, *Resources in Education* (RIE). Most of these publications are available through the
ERIC Document Reproduction Service (EDRS). For publications cited
in this bibliography that are available from EDRS, ordering number
and price code are included. Readers who wish to order a publication should write to the ERIC Document Reproduction Service,
3900 Wheeler Avenue, Alexandria, Virginia 22304. (Phone orders
with VISA or MasterCard are taken at 800/227-ERIC or 703/823-0500.)
When ordering, please specify the document (ED) number. Documents are available as noted in microfiche (MF) and paper copy
(PC). If you have the price code ready when you call EDRS, an exact
price can be quoted. The last page of the latest issue of *Resources
in Education* also has the current cost, listed by code.

Academe. 1987. Special issue on intercollegiate athletics. 73(4).

Alberger, Patti, ed. 1981. *Winning Techniques for Athletic Fund Raising.* Washington, D.C.: Council for Advancement and Support of
Education. ED 208 776. 102 pp. MF–01; PC not available EDRS.

Alfano, Pete. 21 June 1979. "Big-Time Football: Colorado Pays the
Price in Its Quest to Win." *Los Angeles Times.*

American Association of State Colleges and Universities. 1986. *Results
of Survey of AASCU Institutions on Revenues and Expenses of Athletic Programs.* Washington, D.C.: AASCU Committee on Athletics.

American Council on Education. 1979. "Responsibilities in the Conduct of Collegiate Athletics Programs: American Council on Education Policy Statements." *Educational Record* 60(4): 345–50.

Asher, Mark. 10 June 1975. "Play and Not Pay? Maryland's Kehoe
Blasts Title IX, Says Women Can't Produce Income." *Louisville
Courier-Journal.*

———. 12 June 1988. "John Slaughter: Reflections on the Calm after
the Storm." *The Washington Post.*

———. 3 June 1989. "Hard Cash and So Much More: Salary a Pittance
of What Next Maryland Basketball Coach Can Earn." *The Washington Post.*

Associated Press. 5 December 1981. "CFA Not Satisfied." Newport
News–Hampton (Virginia) *Daily Press.*

———. 3 June 1982. "Baliles Questions College Foundations." Newport News–Hampton (Virginia) *Daily Press.*

———. 13 September 1987a. "Giamatti Assails College Athletics."
Newport News–Hampton (Virginia) *Daily Press.*

———. 24 October 1987b. "Ivy Schools Face Unique Limitations."
The Washington Post.

———. 18 November 1987c. "New Image Sought for Virginia Tech." Newport News–Hampton (Virginia) *Daily Press.*

———. 23 November 1987d. "Sports GNP Increases 7 Percent, to $47.2 Billion" Newport News–Hampton (Virginia) *Daily Press.*

———. 27 March 1988a. "NCAA Tournament Has Changed over the Years." Newport News–Hampton (Virginia) *Daily Press.*

———. 11 September 1988b. "University of Michigan Athletic Department Deficits." *The Washington Post.*

———. 4 July 1989a. "Maryland Athletic Director Faces Ethics Probe." Newport News–Hampton (Virginia) *Daily Press.*

———. 18 July 1989b. "Oregon Approves New NFL Lottery: Point-Spread Contest to Help State's College Sports Programs." Newport News–Hampton *Daily Press.*

Association of American Colleges. 1980. *Update on Title IX and Sports.* No. 3. Washington, D.C.: AAC, Project on the Status and Education of Women. ED 187 254. 7 pp. MF–01; PC–01.

Atwell, Robert H. 1979. "Some Reflections on Collegiate Athletics." *Educational Record* 60(4): 367–73.

———. 1985. "It's Only a Game." In *Sport and Higher Education,* edited by Donald Chu, Jeffrey Segrave, and Beverly Becker. Champaign, Ill.: Human Kinetics Publishers.

———. January 1988. "Putting College Sports in Perspective: Solutions for the Long Term." *AAHE Bulletin:* 7–10.

Atwell, Robert H., Bruce Grimes, and Donna A. Lopiano. 1980. *The Money Game: Financing Collegiate Athletics.* Washington, D.C.: American Council on Education.

Balbus, Ike. March 1975. "Politics as Sports: The Political Ascendancy of the Sports Metaphor in America." *Monthly Review:* 26–39.

Baliles, Gerald L. 13 June 1987. "Commencement Address: VPI & SU." Address delivered at Blacksburg, Virginia. Richmond: Commonwealth of Virginia, Office of the Governor.

Barnes, Charlie. 1981. "How a Booster Organization Raises Funds." In *Winning Techniques for Athletic Fund Raising,* edited by Patti Alberger. Washington, D.C.: Council for Advancement and Support of Education. ED 208 776. 102 pp. MF–01; PC not available EDRS.

Barnes, Charlie, Homer Rice, and Ian Sturrock. 1981. "On the Offense: Three Athletic Fund Raisers Tell How They Score." *CASE Currents* 7(11): 12–18.

Bellah, Robert N. Winter 1967. "Civil Religion in America." *Daedalus* 96: 1–21.

Bennett, George. 1981. "Starting from Scratch." In *Winning Techniques for Athletic Fund Raising,* edited by Patti Alberger. Washington, D.C.: Council for Advancement and Support of Education. ED 208 776. 102 pp. MF–01; PC not available EDRS.

Bernstein, Allen. 1986. *1987 Tax Guide for College Teachers and Other College Personnel.* Washington, D.C.: Academic Information

Service.

Bertagna, Joe. 1986. *Crimson in Triumph: A Pictorial History of Harvard Athletics, 1852 to 1985.* Lexington, Mass.: Stephen Greene Press.

Blackburn, Robert T., and Michael S. Nyikos. 1974. "College Football and Mr. Chips: All in the Family." *Phi Delta Kappan* 56(2): 110–13.

Blumenstyk, Goldie. 29 June 1988. "Town-Gown Battles Escalate as Beleaguered Cities Assail College Tax Exemptions." *Chronicle of Higher Education:* A1+.

———. 1 February 1989. "Virginia Governor Advocates More Than an Economic Role for Colleges." *Chronicle of Higher Education:* A15+.

Bok, Derek C. Winter 1980. "The Federal Government and the University." *The Public Interest* 57: 80–101.

———. 1985. "Presidents Need Power within the NCAA to Preserve Academic Standards and Institutional Integrity." In *Sport and Higher Education,* edited by Donald Chu, Jeffrey Segrave, and Beverly Becker. Champaign, Ill.: Human Kinetics Publishers.

Bonk, Thomas. 10 July 1988. "A Winning Formula: UCLA Racks Up the Titles." *Los Angeles Times.*

Boorstin, Daniel J. 1965. "Culture with Many Capitals: The Booster College." In *The Americans: The National Experience.* New York: Random House.

Boyer, Ernest L. 1985. "College Athletics: The Control of the Campus." In *Sport and Higher Education,* edited by Donald Chu, Jeffrey Segrave, and Beverly Becker. Champaign, Ill.: Human Kinetics Publishers.

Brubaker, Bill. 8 February 1988. "The Most Influential Man in the World of High School Basketball?" *The Washington Post.*

Cady, Edwin H. 1978. *The Big Game: College Sports and American Life.* Knoxville: Univ. of Tennessee Press.

Callahan, Bud. 1981. "Endowing the Future." In *Winning Techniques for Athletic Fund Raising,* edited by Patti Alberger. Washington, D.C.: Council for Advancement and Support of Education. ED 208 776. 102 pp. MF–01; PC not available EDRS.

Callahan, Daniel. 25 January 1988. "Developing a Moral Community." Lecture in the series on Professionalism and Ethics in the University Community. Boulder: Univ. of Colorado.

Carlson, Eugene. 28 October 1985. "Little Three Football Is Blocked from TV—By a Little Three Coach." *Wall Street Journal.*

Carnegie Foundation for the Advancement of Teaching. 1982. *The Control of the Campus: A Report on the Governance of Higher Education.* Washington, D.C.: Author.

Childs, Alan W. 1987. "Athletic and Academic Policy in the Context of a New League." *Academe* 73(4): 34–38.

Chu, Donald, Jeffrey Segrave, and Beverly Becker, eds. 1985. *Sport and Higher Education*. Champaign, Ill.: Human Kinetics Publishers.

Clark, Lindley, Jr. 26 August 1986. "The Business of Education: Does Athletics Help or Hurt?" *Wall Street Journal.*

Cohen, Michael D., and James G. March. 1974. *Leadership and Ambiguity: The American College President.* New York: McGraw-Hill.

Combs, Oscar. 24 June 1989. "Athletics Budget to Increase by $1.09 Million for '89-'90." *The Cats' Pause* 13(33): 8.

Conklin, Richard W. 25 September 1978. Letter to the Editor. *Chronicle of Higher Education.*

Cooper, Bob. 16 September 1975. " 'Hidden Man': But Campassi's Vital to UK Attack." Lexington (Kentucky) *Herald-Leader.*

Davenport, Joanna. 1985. "From Crew to Commercialism." In *Sport and Higher Education,* edited by Donald Chu, Jeffrey Segrave, and Beverly Becker. Champaign, Ill.: Human Kinetics Publishers.

Davies, Gordon K. 1987. *Ten Years of Higher Education in Virginia: A Report to the State Council of Higher Education for Virginia.* Richmond: Commonwealth of Virginia.

Davis, William E. 1979. "The President's Role in Athletics: Leader or Figurehead?" *Educational Record* 60(4): 420-30.

Durso, Joseph. 1975. *The Sports Factory: An Investigation into College Sports.* New York: New York Times Book Co.

Educational Record. 1979. Special issue on intercollegiate athletics. 60(4).

El-Khawas, Elaine. 1979. "Self-Regulation and Intercollegiate Athletics." *Educational Record* 60(4): 510-17.

Farrell, Charles S. 8 July 1987. "NCAA Rebuffs Its Presidents' Commission on Proposals to Control Costs of Sports." *Chronicle of Higher Education:* 1+.

Fischer, Norman H. 1975. "Financing of Intercollegiate Athletics: Recommendations." Olympia: Washington State Council on Higher Education. ED 107 172. 85 pp. MF-01; PC-04.

Flexner, Abraham. *Universities: American, English, German.* New York: Oxford Univ. Press, 1930.

Frey, James H. 1985. "College Athletics: Problems of Institutional Control." In *Sport and Higher Education,* edited by Donald Chu, Jeffrey Segrave, and Beverly Becker. Champaign, Ill.: Human Kinetics Publishers.

―――, ed. 1982. *The Governance of Intercollegiate Athletics.* West Point, N.Y.: Leisure Press.

Fullerton, Doug. 1985. "Revenues and Expenses of Intercollegiate Athletics: A Comparison of MSU and Its Peer Campuses." Bozeman: Montana State Univ., Office of Institutional Research. ED 257 330. 30 pp. MF-01; PC-02.

Gerber, Ellen W. 1979. "The Legal Basis for the Regulation of Intercollegiate Sport." *Educational Record* 60(4): 467-81.

Gilbert, Gil. 24 September 1980. "Hold That Tiger: Big Game at Miz-
zou." *Sports Illustrated*: 70–86.

Gilley, J. Wade, and Anthony A. Hickey. 1986. *Administration of University Athletic Programs: Internal Control and Excellence.* Washington, D.C.: American Council on Education. ED 282 481. 66 pp.
MF–01; PC–03.

Glazer, Nathan. Summer 1979. "Regulating Business and the Universities: One Problem or Two?" *The Public Interest* 56: 43–65.

Goodwin, Michael. Fall 1986. "When the Cash Register Is the Score-
board." *The Basketball Bulletin*: 83–86.

Grant, Christine H.B. 1979. "Institutional Autonomy and Intercollegiate Athletics." *Educational Record* 60(4): 409–19.

Green, Madeleine F. 1988. *The American College President: A Contemporary Profile.* Washington, D.C.: American Council on Education. HE 022 128. 43 pp. MF–01; PC–02.

Greene, Linda S. 1984. "The New NCAA Rules of the Game: Academic
Integrity or Racism?" *Saint Louis University Law Journal* 28: 1. ED
242 690. 53 pp. MF–01; PC–03.

Guttmann, Allen. 1982. "The Tiger Devours the Literary Magazine,
or, Intercollegiate Athletics in America." In *The Governance of
Intercollegiate Athletics,* edited by James Frey. West Point, N.Y.:
Leisure Press.

Halstead, Kent H., ed. 1987. *1987 Higher Education Bibliography
Yearbook.* Washington, D.C.: Research Associates.

Hanford, George H. 1974a. *An Inquiry into the Need for and Fea-
sibility of a National Study of Intercollegiate Athletics.* New York:
American Council on Education.

———. 1974b. *The Need for a National Study of Intercollegiate Athletics: A Report to the American Council on Education. Appendices.*
Vol. 2. Washington, D.C.: American Council on Education. ED 132
968. 420 pp. MF–01; PC–17.

———. 1976. "Intercollegiate Athletics Today and Tomorrow: The
President's Challenge." *Educational Record* 57: 232–45.

———. 1979. "Controversies in College Sports." *Educational Record*
60(4): 351–66.

Hardie, Jeff. 4 January 1985. "Virginia Tech Athletics within Shouting
Range of the Best." *The Washington Post.*

Hardy, Stephen H., and Jack W. Berryman. 1982. "A Historical View
of the Governance Issue." In *The Governance of Intercollegiate
Athletics,* edited by James H. Frey. West Point, N.Y.: Leisure Press.

Hart-Nibbrig, Nand, and Clement Cottingham. 1986. *The Political
Economy of College Sports.* Lexington, Mass.: Lexington Books/
D.C. Heath.

Hesburgh, Theodore M. 1977. "The Presidency: A Personalist Manifesto." In *Leadership for Higher Education: The Campus View,*
edited by Roger W. Heyns. Washington, D.C.: American Council

on Education.

Heyman, Ira Michael. September 1987a. "A Modest Proposal." *California Monthly:* 16–18.

———. 1987b. "Trapped in an 'Athletics Arms Race.'" *U.S. News and World Report:* 7.

Higgs, Robert J. 1982. *Sports: A Reference Guide.* Westport, Conn.: Greenwood Press.

Jaschik, Scott. 7 September 1988. "Three More States Adopt Measures to Restrict Campus-Run Businesses." *Chronicle of Higher Education:* A1+.

Jenkins, Sally. 11 May 1985. "Lack of Money Mean Fewer Victories at Maryland." *The Washington Post.*

———. 27 January 1987a. "Maryland Athletic Department Fires Seventeen." *The Washington Post.*

———. 28 January 1987. "Sturtz Holds Meetings to Reassure Maryland Staff: Athletic Director Discusses Budget, Firings." *The Washington Post.*

Journal of College and University Law. 1983–84. Special issue on athletics in higher education. 10(2).

Kaplin, William A. 1985. "Athletics." In *The Law of Higher Education.* San Francisco: Jossey-Bass.

Kauffman, Joseph K. 1980. *At the Pleasure of the Board: The Service of the College and University President.* Washington, D.C.: American Council on Education.

Kerr, Clark. 1963. *The Uses of the University.* Cambridge, Mass.: Harvard Univ. Press.

———. 1982. *The Uses of the University.* 3d ed., with postscript. Cambridge, Mass.: Harvard Univ. Press.

———. 1984. *Presidents Make a Difference: Strengthening Leadership in Colleges and Universities.* Washington, D.C.: Association of Governing Boards. ED 247 879. 140 pp. MF–01; PC not available EDRS.

Kirby, Donald J. March/April 1988. "The Carrier Dome Controversy: Rewriting the Town-Gown Relationship." *Change:* 42-49.

Kjeldsen, Eric K. 1982. "Community Interests and Intercollegiate Athletics." In *The Governance of Intercollegiate Athletics,* edited by James Frey. West Point, N.Y.: Leisure Press.

Koch, James V. September 1971. "The Economics of 'Big-Time' Intercollegiate Athletics." *Social Science Quarterly* 52: 248–60.

Lapchick, Richard. 1987. "The Year Ahead." *Black Issues in Higher Education* 5(11): 4–5.

Lawrence, Paul R. August 1987a. "End Cheating: Pay College Athletes." *Wall Street Journal.*

———. 1987b. *Unsportsmanlike Conduct: The National Collegiate Athletic Association and the Business of College Football.* New York:

Praeger Press.

Lederman, Douglas. 19 November 1986. "The Ivy League at Thirty: A Model for College Athletics or an Outmoded Antique?" *Chronicle of Higher Education:* 1+.

———. 8 July 1987a. "Big-Time College Sports Assailed and Defended at NCAA Forum, but No Consensus Is Reached." *Chronicle of Higher Education:* 32–33.

———. 2 September 1987b. "Rift among Presidents Perils Drive to Reform Big-Time College Sports." *Chronicle of Higher Education:* A92.

———. 29 June 1988a. "College Presidents and Sports Officials Trade Ideas on Athletic Reforms." *Chronicle of Higher Education:* A25.

———. 13 January 1988b. "Do Winning Teams Spur Contributions? Scholars and Fund Raisers Are Skeptical." *Chronicle of Higher Education:* A1+.

———. 21 September 1988c. "Many Public Universities Trying to Assert More Control over Sports Programs Run by Private Associations." *Chronicle of Higher Education:* A41+.

———. 8 June 1988d. "Oregonians Debate Whether to Use Tax Fund to Bolster the State Universities' Flagging Sports Programs." *Chronicle of Higher Education:* A25+.

———. 20 April 1988e. "University of Kentucky's Athletic Association to Provide $4 Million for General Academic Programs." *Chronicle of Higher Education:* A4l+.

———. 31 May 1989. *Chronicle of Higher Education:* A1+.

Lipper, Bob. 6 December 1987. "I-AA Football: Deficits vs. Intangibles." Richmond (Virginia) *Times-Dispatch.*

Looney, Douglas. 6 October 1980. "There Ain't No More Gold in Them Thar Hills." *Sports Illustrated:* 30–37.

Lopiano, Donna A. 1979. "Solving the Financial Crisis in Intercollegiate Athletics." *Educational Record* 60(4): 394–408.

Lowell, Cym H. 1979. "The Law and Intercollegiate Athletics in Public Institutions." *Educational Record* 60(4): 482–98.

Lucey, Gregory F. 1982. "Athletics and Academics: A Case Study in Reassessment." In *The Governance of Intercollegiate Athletics,* edited by James Frey. West Point, N.Y.: Leisure Press.

McCormack, Robert E., and Maurice Tinsley. 1987. "Athletics versus Academics? Evidence from SAT Scores." *Journal of Political Economy* 95(5): 1103–16.

McGuff, Joseph. 11 January 1989. "Spin Doctors of College Athletics Convince Us That All Is Well." *Kansas City Star.*

McMillen, Liz. 14 September 1988. "Reports of Misuse Prompt Widespread Investigations of Public Colleges' Private Fund-Raising Arms." *Chronicle of Higher Education:* A33+.

Maisel, Ivan. 7 June 1988. "CFA Meetings: Talking about Talking." *Dallas Morning News.*

March, James G. 1982. "Emerging Developments in the Study of Organizations." *Review of Higher Education* 6(1): 1–17.

Marx, Jeffrey, and Michael York. 22 December 1985a. "NCAA Can't Agree on How to Clean Up College Sports." Lexington (Kentucky) *Herald-Leader*.

———. 27 and 28 October 1985b. "Playing above the Rules." Lexington (Kentucky) *Herald-Leader*.

Massengale, John D., and John W. Merriman. 1981. *The Administrative Housing of Intercollegiate Athletics: Independent or Affiliated with an Academic Department.* ED 231 779. 17 pp. MF–01; PC–01.

Massengale, Marcy V., ed., and Harry A. Marmion, guest ed. 1979. "On Intercollegiate Athletics." *Educational Record* 60(4).

Merritt, Harry. 22 December 1985. "1985: A Year of Crisis in College Athletics." Lexington (Kentucky) *Herald-Leader*.

Michener, James A. 1976. *Sports in America.* New York: Random House.

Miller, Andy. 1981. "Boosting Athletics with a Separate Club." In *Winning Techniques for Athletic Fund Raising,* edited by Patti Alberger. Washington, D.C.: Council for Advancement and Support of Education. ED 208 776. 102 pp. MF–01; PC not available EDRS.

Miller, Fred L. 1982. "The Athletic Director and the Governance of Sport." In *The Governance of Intercollegiate Athletics,* edited by James Frey. West Point, N.Y.: Leisure Press.

Miller, Richard. 1979. *The Assessment of College Performance.* San Francisco: Jossey-Bass.

Monahan, Bob. 26 June 1980. "Tightening Belts: Like Nearly Everybody, Colleges Are Feeling the Pinch of Inflation." *Los Angeles Times.*

Moore, Kenneth. 20 June 1988. "Giving the Ax to Track: Cutting College Programs Imperils U.S. Olympic Hopes." *Sports Illustrated* 68(25): 84.

Moss, Al. 18 March 1981. "College Football Has a Case of the Shorts." *San Francisco Chronicle.*

Moulton, P. 1978. *Enhancing the Values of Intercollegiate Athletics at Small Colleges.* Ann Arbor: Univ. of Michigan, Center for the Study of Higher Education.

Muller, Steven. 1987. "The University Presidency Today." *Science* 237(4616): 705.

Nader, Samuel J. 1988. "Financing Intercollegiate Athletics in the Southeastern Conference, 1970–1979." Ph.D. dissertation, Louisiana State Univ.

National Collegiate Athletic Association. 1974. *Financial Reporting and Control for Intercollegiate Athletics.* Mission, Kan.: Author.

———. 1981. *The Evaluation of Intercollegiate Athletic Programs: A Suggested Guide for the Process of Self-Study.* Mission, Kan.: Author.

——. 1982. *NCAA Guide for the College-Bound Student-Athlete, 1982-83.* Mission, Kan.: Author.

——. 1985. *1984 NCAA Football Television Committee Report.* Mission, Kan.: Author.

——. 1987. *The Faculty Athletics Representative: A Handbook.* Mission, Kan.: Author.

——. 1989. *1989-90 Manual of the National Collegiate Athletic Association: Constitution, Bylaws, Rules of Order, Executive Regulations, Recommended Policies, Enforcement Procedure, Administration, Case Book.* Mission, Kan.: Author.

Nelson, David M. 1982. "Administrators' Views of Athletic Governance." In *The Governance of Intercollegiate Athletics,* edited by James Frey. West Point, N.Y.: Leisure Press.

Newsom, John. 26 February 1988. "Student Fee Provides Bulk of Athletic Budget." College of William and Mary *Flat Hat:* 6-7.

Nyquist, Ewald B. Fall 1978. "The Future of Collegiate Athletics." *College Board Review* 109: 10-13.

——. 1979. "Win, Women, and Money: Collegiate Athletics Today." *Educational Record* 60(4): 374-93.

Oberlander, Susan. 16 March 1988a. "Big-Time College Football Powers Seek to End Glut of TV Games, Lift Ratings, and Raise Rights Fees." *Chronicle of Higher Education:* A37+.

——. 9 March 1988b. "Chapel Hill Professors Fear That Abuses in Big-Time Sports Upset University's Traditional Athletics-Academics Balance." *Chronicle of Higher Education:* A37+.

——. 20 April 1988c. "New North Carolina Chancellor Has Record of Strong Views on Integrity in Sports." *Chronicle of Higher Education:* A41+.

——. 31 May 1989. "Kentucky Case Shows Cooperation with NCAA Can Head Off Harshest Penalties." *Chronicle of Higher Education:* A1+.

Oliva, L. Jay. 1989. *What Trustees Should Know about Intercollegiate Athletics: AGB Special Report.* Washington, D.C.: Association of Governing Boards.

Padilla, Arthur, and Janice L. Boucher. 1987-88. "On the Economics of Intercollegiate Athletic Programs." *Journal of Sport and Social Issues* 11(1-2): 61-73.

Palmer, Barbara. 1981. "Lobbying the Legislature: How to Win Equity in Athletics." In *Winning Techniques for Athletic Fund Raising,* edited by Patti Alberger. Washington, D.C.: Council for Advancement and Support of Education. ED 208 776. 102 pp. MF-01; PC not available EDRS.

Palmer, Stacey E. 15 June 1988. "College Presidents Warned They Must Make Changes of Substance to Avoid Losing Public's Confidence." *Chronicle of Higher Education:* A7.

Perry, Jean L. 1981. "Future Relationships: Physical Education and Athletics." Paper presented at the Annual Meeting of the American Alliance for Health, Physical Education, Recreation, and Dance, 15 April, Boston, Massachusetts. ED 201 626. 8 pp. MF–01; PC–01.

Radford, Rich. 23 April 1987. "Deficit: Football Program's Losses Unique Investment for W&M." Newport News–Hampton (Virginia) *Daily Press.*

Raiborn, Mitchell H. 1974. *Financial Reporting and Control for Intercollegiate Athletics.* Mission, Kan.: NCAA.

———. 1978. *Revenues and Expenses of Intercollegiate Athletic Programs: Analysis of Financial Trends and Relationships, 1970–1974.* Mission, Kan.: NCAA.

———. 1986. *Revenues and Expenses of Intercollegiate Athletic Programs: Analysis of Financial Trends and Relationships, 1981–85.* Mission, Kan.: NCAA.

Reed, Billy. 20 April 1988. "Big Blue Mentality Has Made Time Stand Still." Lexington (Kentucky) *Herald-Leader.*

Renfro, Wallace I., ed. 1987. *NCAA Faculty Athletics Representatives Forum.* Mission, Kan.: NCAA.

Rice, Homer. 1981. "Athletic Viability: Making It Happen." In *Winning Techniques for Athletic Fund Raising,* edited by Patti Alberger. Washington, D.C.: Council for Advancement and Support of Education. ED 208 776. 102 pp. MF–01; PC not available EDRS.

Riggs, Robert O. 1985. "Auditing the Records of Student-Athletes." *Business Officer* 18(12): 36–38.

Rooney, John F., Jr. 1985. "America Needs a New Intercollegiate Sports System." *Journal of Geography* 84(4): 139–43.

———. 1987. *The Recruiting Game: Toward a New System of Intercollegiate Sport.* 2d ed. Lincoln: Univ. of Nebraska Press.

Rudolph, Frederick. 1962. "The Rise of Football." In *The American College and University: A History.* New York: Random House.

Sack, Allen L. 1982. "CUI BONO? Contradictions in College Sports and Athletes' Rights." In *The Governance of Intercollegiate Athletics,* edited by James Frey. West Point, N.Y.: Leisure Press.

Sage, George H. 1982. "The Intercollegiate Sport Cartel and Its Consequences for Athletes." In *The Governance of Intercollegiate Athletics,* edited by James Frey. West Point, N.Y.: Leisure Press.

Sanford, Terry. 1977. "Cooperative Leadership." In *Leadership for Higher Education: The Campus View,* edited by Roger W. Heyns. Washington, D.C.: American Council on Education.

Sanoff, Alvin P. 11 February 1980. "Behind Scandals in Big-Time College Sports." *U.S. News & World Report:* 61–63.

———. 1 July 1985. "It's Cleanup Time for College Sports." *U.S. News & World Report:* 62–64.

Savage, Howard J., et al. 1929. *American College Athletics.* New York: Carnegie Foundation for the Advancement of Teaching.

Schulian, John. 21 August 1985. "Today's State of Athletics Is a Cancer of Corruption." Newport News–Hampton (Virginia) *Daily Press.*

Scott, H.A. 1956. "New Directions in Intercollegiate Athletics." *Teachers College Record* 38: 29–37.

Sell, David, and Amy Goldstein. 8 February 1989. "Proposal Would Give State Subsidy to College Park Athletics." *The Washington Post.*

Senate Committee on the Judiciary. 1983. *The Collegiate Student-Athlete Protection Act of 1983: Hearings before the Committee on the Judiciary.* Washington, D.C.: Congress of the United States. ED 240 962. 217 pp. MF–01; PC–09.

Sherfey, Michael A. 1980. *Living in the Joe B. Hall Wildcat Lodge: A Personal View of the Kentucky Basketball Program.* Tompkinsville, Ky.: Tompkinsville Publishers.

Sigelman, Lee, and Robert Carter. September 1979. "Win One for the Giver." *Social Science Quarterly* 60: 284–94.

Slosson, Edwin E. 1910. *Great American Universities.* New York: Macmillan.

Southern Association of Colleges and Schools. 1977. *Standards of the College Delegate Assembly.* Atlanta: Commission on Colleges.

———. 1984. *Criteria for Accreditation: Commission on Colleges.* Atlanta: Author.

Sperber, Murray A. 1987. "The College Coach as Entrepreneur." *Academe* 73(4): 30–33.

State Higher Education Executive Officers. 1988. *Funding of Intercollegiate Athletics: Summary of Responses.* Richmond: State Council of Higher Education for Virginia.

Stump, Al. 20 November 1976. "A Happy Athlete Is a Winning Athlete." *TV Guide:* 14–16.

Sturrock, Ian T. 1981. "Chattanooga: Fast Track to Success." In *Winning Techniques for Athletic Fund Raising,* edited by Patti Alberger. Washington, D.C.: Council for Advancement and Support of Education. ED 208 776. 102 pp. MF–01; PC not available EDRS.

Sullivan, Robert. 1987. "Time to Play Foote Ball?" *Sports Illustrated* 67(27): 58–63.

Taaffe, William. 1986. "Why TV Sports Are in Big Trouble." *Sports Illustrated* 64(8): 20–27.

Teel, David. 8 August 1988. "NCAA's Image Worsening Daily." Newport News–Hampton (Virginia) *Daily Press.*

Thelin, John R. 1976. *The Cultivation of Ivy: A Saga of the College in America.* Cambridge, Mass.: Schenkman Publishers.

———. 1978. "Higher Education and Athletics: Probing an American Ethos." *Journal of Educational Thought* 12(3): 176–83.

———. 1981. "Games Colleges Play." *Review of Higher Education* 4(3): 35–43.

———. 1982. "The Sporting Life: Higher Education and Athletics." In *Higher Education and Its Useful Past.* Cambridge, Mass.:

Schenkman Publishers.

———. 1986. "The Campus as Chameleon." In *Higher Education: Handbook of Theory and Research*. New York: Agathon Press.

Thompson, Jack. 1981. "Winning Techniques for Raising Funds." In *Winning Techniques for Athletic Fund Raising*, edited by Patti Alberger. Washington, D.C.: Council for Advancement and Support of Education. ED 208 776. 102 pp. MF–01; PC not available EDRS.

Time. 2 December 1974. "A Majors Success": 84.

Tow, Ted C. 1982. "The Governance Role of the NCAA." In *The Governance of Intercollegiate Athletics*, edited by James Frey. West Point, N.Y.: Leisure Press.

United Press International. 17 June 1982. "Private Contributions Still Big in ACC." Newport News–Hampton (Virginia) *Daily Press*.

University of Kentucky Athletic Association. 1987. *Blue and White Fund*. Lexington, Ky.: Author.

Veysey, Laurence. 1964. *The Emergence of the American University*. Chicago: Univ. of Chicago Press.

Weir, Tom. 13 May 1988. "Hoosiers Losing Knight? Bully for Them!" *USA Today*.

Weistart, John C. 1983–84. "Legal Accountability and the NCAA." *Journal of College and University Law* 10(2): 167–96.

———. 1987. "College Sports Reform: Where Are the Faculty?" *Academe* 73(4): 12–17.

Wilson, Laura A. 1980. "Collegiate Athletics: Views from the Front Office." *Educational Record* 61(4): 2331.

Wiseman, Lawrence W. 1986. "Where Have You Gone, Joe DiMaggio?" *William and Mary Magazine* 54(3): 22–26.

Wong, Glenn M. 1988. *Essentials of Amateur Sports Law*. Dover, Mass.: Auburn Publishing House

INDEX

A

AASCU (see American Association of State Colleges and Universities)

AAU (see Association of American Universities)

ABC Sports, 55, 57

Abuses (see Scandals)

Academe, 4

Academic departments: comparison with sports, 15, 99

Academic reform model, 100–101

Academics
    and athletics, 28–32, 63–64, 89, 100–101, 103
    criteria for freshmen, 71
    policy, 34
    standards, 25, 101

ACC (see Atlantic Coast Conference)

Accountability
    nonprofit status, 51
    reform, 101–103
    to university, 35, 96

Accreditation
    agencies, 69
    athletics, 102–103
    standards, 34–41, 96, 102

ACE (see American Council on Education)

Admissions, 101

AGB (see Association of Governing Boards of Universities and Colleges)

All-star games, 57

Alumni
    booster club members, 28
    donations, 19, 22, 26, 28–30

American Association of State Colleges and Universities (AASCU), 39, 51

American Council on Education (ACE), 4, 70, 71

Amherst College, 5, 23

Antitrust laws, 56

ASHE (see Association for the Study of Higher Education)

Assessment of College Performance, 3

Associated Press polls, 77

Association for the Study of Higher Education (ASHE), 3

Association of American Universities (AAU), 30

Association of Governing Boards of Universities and Colleges (AGB), 4, 34

Athletes
    academic criteria, 71
    isolation, 100
    research need, 10
    SAT scores, 2

"Athletics arms race," 22

Rules
> bending, 5
> NCAA changes, 70–74, 83

S

Salaries
> athletes, 36
> coaches, 22
> faculty, 31, 40

SAT scores
> athletes', 2
> increase in, 29

Sanctions, 83, 101–102

Sanford, Terry, 80

Scandals
> associated with winning teams, 29
> "death penalty," 78
> effects, 60, 70, 101
> gubernatorial reaction, 61
> slush funds, 51, 57
> indictments/denials, 7
> national publicity, 2–3
> public confidence, 79–80

Scholarship
> studies, 3
> trends, 4–5

Scholarships (see also Grants-in-aid)
> abolition, 21
> Division III, 69
> redefinition, 36

Scholastic Aptitude Tests (see SAT scores)

SEC (see Southeastern Conference)

Self-supporting programs
> definition, 39
> major universities, 5

Seminole Boosters Club, 34

SHEEO (see State Higher Education Executive Officers)

Shoe companies, 57–58

Slaughter, John, 73, 76, 77, 78

Slush funds, 34, 51, 57

Small colleges, 5, 23, 69

"Smokeless industry," 44

Southeastern Conference (SEC)
> ban against playing in, 18
> financial reform, 20–21
> fund raising, 27
> rule bending, 5,
> status, 17, 24

Since 1983, the Association for the Study of Higher Education (ASHE) and the Educational Resources Information Center (ERIC) Clearinghouse on Higher Education, a sponsored project of the School of Education and Human Development at The George Washington University, have cosponsored the *ASHE-ERIC Higher Education Report* series. The 1989 series is the eighteenth overall and the first to be published by the School of Education and Human Development at the George Washington University.

Each monograph is the definitive analysis of a tough higher education problem, based on thorough research of pertinent literature and insitutional experiences. Topics are identified by a national survey. Noted practitioners and scholars are then commissioned to write the reports, with experts providing critical reviews of each manuscript before publication.

Eight monographs (10 before 1985) in the ASHE-ERIC Higher Education Report series are published each year and are available on a individual or subscription basis. Subscription to eight issues is $80.00 annually; $60 to members of AAHE, AIR, or AERA; and $50 to ASHE members. All foreign subscribers must include an additional $10 per series year for postage.

Prices for single copies, including book rate postage, are $15.00 regular and $11.25 for members of AERA, AIR, AAHE, and ASHE ($10.00 regular and $7.50 for members for 1985 to 1987 reports, $7.50 regular and $6.00 for members for 1983 and 1984 reports, $6.50 regular and $5.00 for members for reports published before 1982). All foreign orders must include $1.00 per book for foreign postage. Fast United Parcel Service or first class postage is available for $1.00 per book in the U.S. and $2.50 per book outside the U.S. (orders above $50.00 may substitue 5% of the total invoice amount for domestic postage). Make checks payable to ASHE-ERIC. For VISA and MasterCard payments, include card number, expiration date, and signature. Orders under $25 must be prepaid. Bulk discounts are avilable on order of 15 or more reports (not applicable to subscription orders). Order from the Publications Department, ASHE-ERIC Higher Education Reports, The George Washington University, One Dupont Circle, Suite 630, Washington, DC 20036-1183, or phone us at (202) 296-2597. Write for a complete catalog of all available reports.

1989 ASHE-ERIC Higher Education Reports

1. Making Sense of Administrative Leadership: The 'L' Word in Higher Education
   Estela M. Bensimon, Anna Neumann, and Robert Birnbaum

2. Affirmative Rhetoric, Negative Action: African-American and Hispanic Faculty at Predominantly White Universities
   Valora Washington and William Harvey

3. Postsecondary Developmental Programs: A Traditional Agenda with New Imperatives
   Louise M. Tomlinson

4. The Old College Try: Balancing Athletics and Academics in Higher Education
   John R. Thelin and Lawrence L. Wiseman

1988 ASHE-ERIC Higher Education Reports

1. The Invisible Tapestry: Culture in American Colleges and Universities
   George D. Kuh and Elizabeth J. Whitt

2. Critical Thinking: Theory, Research, Practice, and Possibilities
   Joanne Gainen Kurfiss

3. Developing Academic Programs: The Climate for Innovation
   Daniel T. Seymour

4. Peer Teaching: To Teach is To Learn Twice
   Neal A. Whitman

5. Higher Education and State Governments: Renewed Partnership, Cooperation, or Competition?
   Edward R. Hines

6. Entrepreneurship and Higher Education: Lessons for Colleges, Universities, and Industry
   James S. Fairweather

7. Planning for Microcomputers in Higher Education: Strategies for the Next Generation
   Reynolds Ferrante, John Hayman, Mary Susan Carlson, and Harry Phillips

8. The Challenge for Research in Higher Education: Harmonizing Excellence and Utility
   Alan W. Lindsay and Ruth T. Neumann

1987 ASHE-ERIC Higher Education Reports

1. Incentive Early Retirement Programs for Faculty: Innovative Responses to a Changing Environment
   Jay L. Chronister and Thomas R. Kepple, Jr.

2. Working Effectively with Trustees: Building Cooperative Campus Leadership
   Barbara E. Taylor

3. Formal Recognition of Employer-Sponsored Instruction: Conflict and Collegiality in Postsecondary Education
   Nancy S. Nash and Elizabeth M. Hawthorne

4. Learning Styles: Implications for Improving Educational Practices
   Charles S. Claxton and Patricia H. Murrell

5. Higher Education Leadership: Enhancing Skills through Professional Development Programs
   Sharon A. McDade
6. Higher Education and the Public Trust: Improving Stature in Colleges and Universities
   Richard L. Alfred and Julie Weissman
7. College Student Outcomes Assessment: A Talent Development Perspective
   Maryann Jacobi, Alexander Astin, and Frank Ayala, Jr.
8. Opportunity from Strength: Strategic Planning Clarified with Case Examples
   Robert G. Cope

1986 ASHE-ERIC Higher Education Reports

1. Post-tenure Faculty Evaluation: Threat or Opportunity?
   Christine M. Licata
2. Blue Ribbon Commissions and Higher Education: Changing Academe from the Outside
   Janet R. Johnson and Laurence R. Marcus
3. Responsive Professional Education: Balancing Outcomes and Opportunities
   Joan S. Stark, Malcolm A. Lowther, and Bonnie M.K. Hagerty
4. Increasing Students' Learning: A Faculty Guide to Reducing Stress among Students
   Neal A. Whitman, David C. Spendlove, and Claire H. Clark
5. Student Financial Aid and Women: Equity Dilemma?
   Mary Moran
6. The Master's Degree: Tradition, Diversity, Innovation
   Judith S. Glazer
7. The College, the Constitution, and the Consumer Student: Implications for Policy and Practice
   Robert M. Hendrickson and Annette Gibbs
8. Selecting College and University Personnel: The Quest and the Question
   Richard A. Kaplowitz

1985 ASHE-ERIC Higher Education Reports

1. Flexibility in Academic Staffing: Effective Policies and Practices
   Kenneth P. Mortimer, Marque Bagshaw, and Andrew T. Masland
2. Associations in Action: The Washington, D.C. Higher Education Community
   Harland G. Bloland

3. And on the Seventh Day: Faculty Consulting and Supplemental Income
   Carol M. Boyer and Darrell R. Lewis

4. Faculty Research Performance: Lessons from the Sciences and Social Sciences
   John W. Creswell

5. Academic Program Review: Institutional Approaches, Expectations, and Controversies
   Clifton F. Conrad and Richard F. Wilson

6. Students in Urban Settings: Achieving the Baccalaureate Degree
   Richard C. Richardson, Jr. and Louis W. Bender

7. Serving More Than Students: A Critical Need for College Student Personnel Services
   Peter H. Garland

8. Faculty Participation in Decision Making: Necessity or Luxury?
   Carol E. Floyd

1984 ASHE-ERIC Higher Education Reports

1. Adult Learning: State Policies and Institutional Practices
   K. Patricia Cross and Anne-Marie McCartan

2. Student Stress: Effects and Solutions
   Neal A. Whitman, David C. Spendlove, and Claire H. Clark

3. Part-time Faulty: Higher Education at a Crossroads
   Judith M. Gappa

4. Sex Discrimination Law in Higher Education: The Lessons of the Past Decade
   J. Ralph Lindgren, Patti T. Ota, Perry A. Zirkel, and Nan Van Gieson

5. Faculty Freedoms and Institutional Accountability: Interactions and Conflicts
   Steven G. Olswang and Barbara A. Lee

6. The High Technology Connection: Academic/Industrial Cooperation for Economic Growth
Lynn G. Johnson

7. Employee Educational Programs: Implications for Industry and Higher Education
   Suzanne W. Morse

8. Academic Libraries: The Changing Knowledge Centers of Colleges and Universities
   Barbara B. Moran

9. Futures Research and the Strategic Planning Process: Implications for Higher Education
   James L. Morrison, William L. Renfro, and Wayne I. Boucher

10. Faculty Workload: Research, Theory, and Interpretation
   Harold E. Yuker

1983 ASHE-ERIC Higher Education Reports

1. The Path to Excellence: Quality Assurance in Higher Education
   Laurence R. Marcus, Anita O. Leone, and Edward D. Goldberg

2. Faculty Recruitment, Retention, and Fair Employment: Obligations and Opportunities
   John S. Waggaman

3. Meeting the Challenges: Developing Faculty Careers*
   Michael C.T. Brooks and Katherine L. German

4. Raising Academic Standards: A Guide to Learning Improvement
   Ruth Talbott Keimig

5. Serving Learners at a Distance: A Guide to Program Practices
   Charles E. Feasley

6. Competence, Admissions, and Articulation: Returning to the Basics in Higher Education
   Jean L. Preer

7. Public Service in Higher Education: Practices and Priorities
   Patricia H. Crosson

8. Academic Employment and Retrenchment: Judicial Review and Administrative Action
   Robert M. Hendrickson and Barbara A. Lee

9. Burnout: The New Academic Disease*
   Winifred Albizu Meĺendez and Rafael M. de Guzmán

10. Academic Workplace: New Demands, Heightened Tensions
   Ann E. Austin and Zelda F. Gamson

*Out-of-print. Available through EDRS. Call 1-800-227-ERIC.

ORDER FORM

Quantity   **Amount**

_____ Please begin my subscription to the 1989 *ASHE-ERIC Higher Education Reports* at $80.00, 33% off the cover price, starting with Report 1, 1989   _____

_____ Please begin my subscription to the 1990 *ASHE-ERIC Higher Education Reports* at $80.00 starting with Report 1, 1990   _____

_____ Outside the U.S., add $10 per series for postage   _____

Individual reports are avilable at the following prices:

1988 and forward, $15	1983 and 1984, $7.50
1985 to 1987, $10	1982 and back, $6.50

Book rate postage within the U.S. is included. Outside U.S., please add $1 per book for postage. Fast U.P.S. shipping is available within the U.S. at $1 per book; outside the U.S., $2.50 per book; orders over $50 may add 5% of the invoice total. All orders under $25 must be prepaid.

PLEASE SEND ME THE FOLLOWING REPORTS:

Quantity	Report No.	Year	Title	Amount

Subtotal:	
Postage(optional):	
Total Due:	

Please check one of the following:
- ☐ Check enclosed, payable to GWU-ERIC.
- ☐ Purchase order attached.
- ☐ Charge my credit card indicated below:
- ☐ Visa   ☐ MasterCard

[ ][ ][ ][ ][ ][ ][ ][ ][ ][ ][ ][ ][ ][ ][ ][ ]

Expiration Date _____

Name _____

Title _____

Institution _____

Address _____

City _____ State _____ Zip _____

Phone _____

Signature _____

SEND ALL ORDERS TO:
ASHE-ERIC Higher Education Reports
The George Washington University
One Dupont Circle, Suite 630
Washington, DC 20036-1183
Phone: (202) 296-2597